The
Professional
Nanny

The Professional Nanny

MONICA M. BASSETT, R.N.

Cuyahoga Community College
Founder, Nannies of Cleveland

Delmar Publishers

an International Thomson Publishing company I(T)P®

Albany • Bonn • Boston • Cincinnati • Detroit • London • Madrid
Melbourne • Mexico City • New York • Pacific Grove • Paris
San Francisco • Singapore • Tokyo • Toronto • Washington

NOTICE TO THE READER

Cover Design: Brucie Rosch

Delmar Staff
Publisher: William Brottmiller
Senior Editor: Jay Whitney
Associate Editor: Erin J. O'Connor Traylor
Production Coordinator: James Zayicek
Art and Design Coordinator: Carol D. Keohane
Editorial Assistant: Ellen Smith

Copyright © 1998
by Delmar Publishers
a division of International Thomson Publishing Inc.

The ITP logo is a trademark under license.

Printed in the United States of America

For more information, contact:

Delmar Publishers
3 Columbia Circle, Box 15015
Albany, New York 12212-5015

International Thomson Publishing
Europe
Berkshire House 168-173
High Holborn
London, WC1V 7AA
England

Thomas Nelson Australia
102 Dodds Street
South Melbourne, 3205
Victoria, Australia

Nelson Canada
1120 Birchmont Road
Scarborough, Ontario
Canada, M1K 5G4

International Thomson Editores
Campos Eliseos 385, Piso 7
Col Polanco
11560 Mexico D F Mexico

International Thomson Publishing GmbH
Konigswinterer Strasse 418
53227 Bonn
Germany

International Thomson Publishing Asia
221 Henderson Road
#05-10 Henderson Building
Singapore 0315

International Thomson Publishing—Japan
Hirakawacho Kyowa Building, 3F
2-2-1 Hirakawacho
Chiyoda-ku, Tokyo 102
Japan

1 2 3 4 5 6 7 8 9 10 XXX 02 01 00 99 98 97

Library of Congress Cataloging-in-Publication Data

Bassett, Monica M.
    The professional nanny / Monica M. Bassett.
       p.   cm.
    Includes bibliographical references and index.
    ISBN 0-8273-7384-8
    1. Nannies—United States—Vocational guidance. I. Title.
HQ778.63.B38 1997
649'.1'02373—dc21
                                97-7422
                                CIP

To Ben
for his never-failing patience, humor, and help.

Contents

Preface

This is a career handbook for those in the field of early care and education who have chosen to work with young children and their families in private homes as nannies. Although nannies share many ideals, knowledge, and skills with other child-care practitioners, they encounter some unique situations because their employment setting is the private home. Ten years of experience with nanny training and placement have convinced me that success as a nanny depends not only on being skillful with children, but on understanding the professional and business side of nanny employment.

The purpose of this handbook is to provide the basic information a nanny needs to work effectively with an employing family. The book is simple and nontechnical in style. Practical application of material is emphasized. Research documentation, typical of most textbooks, has been intentionally omitted. However, information is based on relevant resources currently available and reflected in each chapter's bibliography.

For those who are entering the field of in-home child care or those who are already in practice, this book is intended to be a resource and guide. It is designed to serve as a text for nanny professionalism courses in nanny training programs or when offered as an option in early childhood education or related programs.

Beginning with the foundations of nanny professionalism in an historical context, the handbook explores the nanny's role and responsibilities when working with today's families. Among the many topics discussed are: professional relationships, ethics, commitment to children, the challenges and rewards of working in a private home, communications, taking care of one's own well-being as a nanny, social skills, travel, the process of seeking a nanny position, employer responsibilities, the nanny job description and written employment agreement, starting and leaving a job. Child abuse, domestic violence, drug abuse, and sexual harassment are also covered.

Useful features of this book include sample forms such as the written employment agreement and the daily log. Books for further reading on topics of particular interest or for the nanny's own professional library are suggested in an annotated list. Additional resources such as organizations and agencies are also included for nannies and families. Terms with which the nanny should become familiar are listed at the beginning of each chapter and defined both at the foot of the page where they appear in the text and in a glossary.

An accompanying instructor's guide identifies competencies to be developed and provides lesson outlines and test questions. Class activities are designed to stimulate consideration of real-life situations and experiences in nanny employment.

Gender-neutral language is used almost exclusively, but where pronouns are unavoidable, he and she are alternated in preference to the cumbersome he/she format.

Offering a career alternative to child-care practitioners, skilled in-home care also provides another option to parents seeking quality care for their children. This book reflects my belief that becoming a professional nanny is an important specialty within the field of early care and education.

Author's Note

Information in this book is not intended as a substitute for proper medical, legal, or other professional advice that the reader should seek as appropriate and necessary.

About the Author

Monica M. Bassett, R.N., B.A.

Monica Bassett brings her nursing background to the early childhood field where her particular interest is training for child-care practitioners. She grew up in England and graduated from Guy's Hospital School of Nursing, London. She also holds a degree in social science from Baldwin Wallace College. As a nursing instructor in maternal-infant health, she worked with students, parents, and infants for many years before developing a nanny training program to improve the quality of in-home child care available to families. She established Nannies of Cleveland School and directed the program from 1985–1992. A founding member of the International Nanny Association, she served as an officer during the Association's early years.

Retired now from directly training nannies, Monica Bassett has turned to writing as another way to promote the well-being of young children and is the author of *Infant and Child Care Skills* (Delmar 1995). She teaches child health and development at Cuyahoga Community College and trains teachers in child-care centers. She is a consultant to educators and parents, specializing in nanny training and practice. She has made many presentations to academic, professional, and community groups. Parenting five children of her own and becoming a grandmother have added a personal dimension to her appreciation of what is involved in caring for children.

Acknowledgments

There are many who made this book possible. I am grateful to my family, friends, and colleagues from whose inspiration, abilities, and support I have benefited. Deborah Davis deserves a special mention for convening the first International Nanny Conference in 1986 and providing a forum for nanny ideas and information in the *National Nanny Newsletter*. I also learned much that has been useful in developing this book from the students of Nannies of Cleveland School and the families who employed them after graduation.

I am particularly indebted to Becky Wyatt and Terry Gaston of Murray State College, Tishomingo, Oklahoma, who graciously provided photographs of the College's nanny program for the book.

My appreciation goes to Jay Whitney and Erin O'Connor Traylor at Delmar Publishers for their guidance throughout this project. Thanks are due to Glenna Stanfield who was always there when I had a question. Special acknowledgement goes to Delmar's reviewers for their thoughtful comments and helpful suggestions.

Alicia Baillie
Southeast Community College
Lincoln, NE

Alison Critchfield
Midway College
Midway, KY

Jan Hodson
Hocking College, Nanny Academy
Nelsonville, OH

Marjorie Judson
Carl Sandberg College
Galesburg, IL

Linda D. Riepe
Lane Community College
Eugene, OR

Last, but by no means least, I want to thank my husband, Ben, to whom this book is dedicated. For many reasons, I could not have written it without him.

Monica M. Bassett

Chapter 1

Introduction to In-Home Child Care

TOPICS

- ◆ Introduction
- ◆ Defining Child Care
- ◆ History of the Nanny
- ◆ Definitions of In-Home Child-Care Providers
- ◆ Contemporary American Nannies

- ◆ Advantages and Disadvantages of In-Home Child Care
- ◆ The Larger Early Childhood Community

Terms to Know

development

nanny

self-worth

Victorian

Middle Ages

manners

wet nurse

rocker

Industrial Revolution

governess

nursery nurse

professional

au pair

tutor

newborn

infant

kindergarten

INTRODUCTION

Caring for young children is a challenging and rewarding occupation regardless of where care is given. Children's needs are the same whether they are cared for in child-care centers, family day-care homes, or in their own homes. All caregivers must have a genuine interest in promoting children's well-being and possess the skills necessary to nurture healthy **development**. In addition, specialized skills are needed depending on the caregiver's employment situation. This book examines the specialized skills needed by caregivers when they are employed as nannies in private homes.

In-home child care has its own history and tradition within the early childhood field. This chapter is designed to acquaint you with the history of the **nanny** and the nanny's place in the larger early childhood community today.

---

development—Series of changes that occur with passing time in an orderly sequence and with the integration of biological and environmental factors.

nanny—In-home caregiver employed by a family, either on a live-in or live-out basis, to perform all tasks related to the care of young children. Implies a caregiver with special training or considerable experience. Sometimes referred to as a child's nurse.

DEFINING CHILD CARE

During the early years of childhood, care and education go hand in hand. Children cannot learn and thrive if their physical needs are not met. However, meeting physical needs is not enough for healthy development. From birth, care must be provided in responsive, respectful ways that help the child develop a sense of security and **self-worth**. Even as young children are having their physical needs met, they are learning about the world and the people in it. Everyday routines and play offer a rich array of opportunities for the young child to experiment, discover, and learn. Child care, therefore, encompasses all activities performed by the caregiver, including physical care, measures to promote health and safety, caring for the sick child, and facilitating educational stimulation and play (Figure 1-1).

HISTORY OF THE NANNY

Great Britain

The term "nanny" is used for a person who takes care of someone else's child in the child's own home (see pages 9 and 10 for definitions of terms used for various in-home caregivers). The origin of the word is obscure. The title was in use in the eighteenth century. It may come from "Nan," a diminutive form of the name "Ann" or "Anna," a popular name in England for centuries. In **Victorian** England, "nanny" was in common usage and used interchangeably with "nurse" to refer to the person in the household who took care of the children. "Nanny" or "nana" may have derived from young children's attempts to say "nurse." In *A Child's Garden of Verses*, Robert Louis Stevenson refers to his nurse/nanny in several poems. Her name was Alison Cunningham and the book was dedicated to her (1905).

---

self-worth—How a person values himself or herself.

Victorian—Characteristic of the period when Victoria was queen of England, 1837–1901.

Figure 1.1 In early childhood, care and education go hand in hand.
(Courtesy Murray State College, Tishomingo, Oklahoma)

Few records of childrearing practices exist until the late **Middle Ages**. Historically, children were viewed as small adults requiring no special consideration. For those who managed to survive the early years at a time when there was little protection against disease, childhood was short. Whether of noble or com-

---

Middle Ages—The period of European history between ancient and modern times, from about the fifth to the fifteenth century A.D.

mon birth, children of about seven years of age began their training in the skills and **manners** needed for their place in adult society. This could involve being sent away from the parental home to serve an apprenticeship in another household. As infants, they were often looked after by servants or older members of the household.

The practice of wealthy women employing **wet nurses** to breastfeed and care for their babies was common in Europe from the Middle Ages to the eighteenth century when it declined. With no safe alternative to breastfeeding, mothers who could not or did not want to feed their babies put them in the care of women whose own babies had died recently. Juliet's nurse in Shakespeare's *Romeo and Juliet* was a wet nurse during Juliet's infancy and her companion and confidante as Juliet grew up.

A type of servant hired specifically for child-care-related tasks was the **rocker**. Often as young as twelve, the rocker's position in the household was a lowly one. She was employed to perform menial tasks and rock the baby's cradle. By the nineteenth century the rocker seems to have disappeared from use, replaced by the nursery maid.

Beginning in the mid-eighteenth century, England underwent significant economic and social changes because of the **Industrial Revolution**. Wealth and population increased. A separate nursery, presided over by a children's nurse or nanny, became increasingly common. Children and parents led separate lives, seeing each other only for a brief, arranged visit each day. At about age seven, children were transferred from the care of the

---

manners—Polite behavior in accordance with social conventions and consideration for others.

wet nurse—A woman employed to breastfeed another woman's baby.

rocker—Servant hired to rock the baby's cradle.

Industrial Revolution—Profound changes in social and economic organization, beginning in England around 1760, as machines replaced hand tools and large-scale industrial production developed.

nanny in the nursery to the supervision of a **governess** in the schoolroom, or they were sent away to boarding school.

By the nineteenth century, Great Britain was one of the wealthiest countries in the world. Middle- and upper-class families employed increasing numbers of servants. The nanny held a respected place in the household and enjoyed higher social status than other domestic employees. The nursery, often located on the upper floor of the house, was her domain. Her charges were cared for according to her childrearing methods. In large households, the head nanny had her own staff, which might include an under nanny and one or more nursery maids. A fortunate nursery maid might rise in the ranks to become an under nanny and perhaps eventually a head nanny.

Life in the Victorian nursery was very regulated. Meals were plain, discipline strict, and punishment sometimes harsh. Children were not pampered, even in wealthy families. The emphasis was on their physical care, with little regard shown for their emotional development. Nevertheless, the nanny was a very important person in the lives of the children in her care. Winston Churchill and Robert Louis Stevenson are among many who were brought up by a nanny with whom they developed a deep, affectionate bond. For Stevenson, his nanny was "the angel of my infant life." Some nannies remained with the same families for life, caring for the children and grandchildren of their original charges.

There was no opportunity for formal nanny or **nursery nurse** training until 1892 when Mrs. Walter Ward founded Norland Nursery Training College (known as Norland Institute at its founding). Until then, under nannies and nursery maids were trained by the experienced head nanny under whose supervision they worked. A teacher herself, and a teacher of teachers, Mrs.

---

governess—A woman employed by a family as a teacher to educate school-age children at home. Male equivalent: **tutor**.

nursery nurse—Title given in Great Britain to a person who has received special training and is qualified to care for young children in group settings as well as private homes.

Ward was influenced by Fredrich Froebel (1782–1852), a pioneer in the field of early childhood education. She promoted Froebel's ideas, revolutionary at the time, that children's first educational experiences should be through play and discovery and that childhood should be pleasant. Aware of the oppressive methods used by many nannies, Mrs. Ward realized that there was a need for educated women to care for young children as nursery nurses and that this offered another career opportunity besides school teaching for young women of genteel birth.

Mrs. Ward's colleagues in education were not enthusiastic about her proposal to establish a nursery nurse training program. Doubts were raised about the employability of trained nannies on the one hand and about the difficulties of recruiting students on the other. Undaunted, Mrs. Ward persevered with her plans and, by founding the Norland Institute, introduced the concept of the child-care **professional**. The trained nanny proved to be so successful that by 1920, 30 more private training colleges had been established in Great Britain. In 1992, Norland celebrated 100 years of nursery nurse training.

The social and economic changes resulting from World War II (1939–1945) led to a decline in the employment of nannies by British families. Many training colleges closed. However, the war created the need for more group child-care programs to allow young mothers to enter the workforce as replacements for men in the armed forces and to care for children moved away from their homes in big cities to avoid bombing. These day and residential nurseries were generally staffed by women trained through an in-service program of the National Society of Children's Nurseries, founded in 1906. In 1945, the National Nursery Examination Board (NNEB) was established to develop a national examination and certificate for all nursery nurse students. Training programs leading to the NNEB qualification became available in public as well as private colleges. Graduates of these programs, then as now, work in day-care

---

professional—One who engages in an occupation requiring special preparation and competencies; pertaining to a profession.

centers, nursery schools, residential nurseries and hospitals, as well as in private homes as nannies.

In the years following the war, British mothers, like their American counterparts, tended to stay at home with their children rather than go out to work. Families who could afford help with child care in the home usually relied on a mother's helper or an **au pair**, but did not leave the children in her sole charge. In the late 1970s, increasing numbers of women chose to combine careers outside the home with motherhood. The demand for nannies returned and has continued to the present.

In 1994, the National Nursery Examination Board merged with another organization, the Council for Early Years Awards, to form the Council for Awards in Children's Care and Education.

America

As in England, American families who could afford servants were likely to entrust the care of their children to them for a good portion of time. In the North, families that accumulated great wealth as the result of industrialization were able to employ British nannies. Separate nurseries, strict routines, and a daily visit of about an hour with their parents characterized the lives of nineteenth century upper-class children in America.

Prior to the Civil War, children of plantation owners in the South were cared for by enslaved black nursemaids. Some plantation families employed a governess or **tutor** from the North to educate older children or sent their children away to boarding school.

For upper-class American families, the custom of employing a nanny became a part of their way of life. The custom remained

---

au pair—*Person who lives as part of a host family in a foreign country to experience the culture and improve skills in the country's language in return for helping with child care and housework. French term literally meaning "as an equal."*

tutor—*A man employed by a family as a teacher to educate school-age children at home. Female equivalent: governess.*

limited to the upper class until the early 1980s when increasing numbers of professional women began to enter the paid work force, combining marriage, motherhood, and a career. Two-career families became the new employers of nannies. They discovered that a nanny suited their child-care needs. A lack of nanny tradition in the United States and immigration laws restricting the entry of trained foreign nannies into the country created the need for the American nanny to meet this new demand for nannies. The "nanny movement" was launched.

The 1980s saw the establishment of the first nanny training programs in the United States in colleges, vocational/technical schools, and private career schools. Nanny placement agencies also proliferated. In 1986, Dr. Deborah Davis, editor of the National Nanny Newsletter, organized the first International Nanny Conference. It was held at Scripps College in California and attended by nannies, nanny educators, agencies, and employers. The International Nanny Association (INA) was an outgrowth of the conference, and in the years following, other organizations were formed to focus on the individual interests of nannies, educators and agencies (see Appendix D for nanny resources, including organizations).

DEFINITIONS OF IN-HOME CHILD-CARE PROVIDERS

The United States does not yet have a standardized nanny certificate program to distinguish the professional nanny or nursery nurse from other types of in-home caregivers. In 1988, the International Nanny Association adopted the following definitions and job descriptions for in-home child-care providers:

Babysitter: Provides supervisory custodial care for children on an irregular full-time or part-time basis. No special training or background expected.

Au Pair: 1) European. Foreign nationals in the United States for up to a year to learn English for cultural purposes. Lives as part of host family and for small allowance/salary helps with housework and child care. May or may not have prior child-care experience. 2) American. Lives with family and provides help with light housework and child care 45 to 50 hours a week. Usually works under the supervision and direction of the parent(s). May or may not have prior child-care experience.

Parent/Mother's Helper: Lives in or out and works for a family to provide full-time child care and other domestic help for families in which one parent is home most of the time. Usually works under the direction and supervision of the at-home parent, but may be left in complete charge for brief periods. No special training is expected.

Nanny: Employed by a family on either a live-in or live-out basis to undertake all tasks related to the care of children. Duties are generally restricted to child care and the domestic tasks related to child care. May or may not have had any formal training, though often has a good deal of actual experience. Nanny's work week ranges from 40 to 60 hours a week. Usually works unsupervised.

Nursery Nurse: The title used in Britain for a person who has received special training and preparation in caring for young children (not limited to in-home care). When employed by a family, may live in or out; works independently and is responsible for everything related to the care of the children in her charge. Duties are generally restricted to child care and the domestic tasks related to child care. Work week is usually 50 to 60 hours per week. In addition to specialized training, the nursery nurse will have passed the national certification examination of the National Nursery Examination Board (and has an N.N.E.B. certificate).

Governess: Traditionally, an educationally qualified person employed by families for the full or part-time at-home education of school-age children. Teaches children and is not usually concerned with domestic work or the physical care of younger children. Hours of work by arrangement.

(Courtesy International Nanny Association.)

CONTEMPORARY AMERICAN NANNIES

In the past 15 years or so, the nanny has emerged as a viable child-care alternative for families and an employment option in the field of early care and education.

Modern American nannies, unlike their Victorian predecessors, do not rule over nurseries that separate the children's lives from the parents' lives. Nor are they usually members of a large household staff. Today's American nannies are most likely to work for two-career parents who perceive the nanny as part of a team dedicated to promoting their children's healthy development. Some nannies live in their employer's homes, while others have homes of their own and commute to work each day. Nannies also take positions in families where there is only one parent.

Although nannies are usually associated with full-time, on-going employment with one family, they sometimes take part-time or temporary positions. The skills of a nanny can be of value to a family when a parent is ill and in-home care is needed temporarily, or when parents want to take a trip together without the children. Parents sometimes require in-home child care just in the summer months when school-age children are on vacation, or when a child comes to visit a non-custodial parent. Some nannies specialize in **newborn** care and assist families during the first few weeks following the birth of a baby.

It is difficult to determine how many nannies are employed in the United States at present. According to the U.S. Census Bureau, data collected in the fall of 1991 indicated that 5.3 percent of children under five years whose mothers were employed were cared for in their own homes by a nonrelative (522,262 children).

---

newborn—The infant during the first four weeks after birth. Also called a neonate.

ADVANTAGES AND DISADVANTAGES OF IN-HOME CHILD CARE

Families and caregivers need to consider both the advantages and disadvantages of in-home child care, so that an employment situation is entered into with realistic expectations and steps can be taken to avoid or minimize possible drawbacks.

One of the greatest benefits that in-home child care offers is stability. Children remain in familiar surroundings with their own toys and with no disruption to the daily routine. They are in the care of one constant person while parents are away. They do not have to be ready to leave the house at a certain time every day to go to the child-care center or family day-care provider. Parents do not have to schedule transportation to and from the child-care site into their daily routines.

A nanny is able to provide the kind of individualized care that is hard to achieve when caring for a group of young children. Specialized care from a consistent caregiver is especially important for building a sense of security and trust in babies. Not all child-care centers have **infant** programs, and when they do, there may not be sufficient caregivers to provide the personal attention babies need.

Children cared for in their own homes are less exposed to infectious illnesses than children in group settings. Furthermore, when a child in group care is ill, parents have to take time off from work to care for the child at home or arrange for substitute care. When the care is in the home, the nanny is available to look after the child who becomes ill.

A nanny has the opportunity to know the child in the context of the child's family and to learn more about the child's world than is usually possible in group settings. This provides the nanny with valuable background for planning appropriate care for the particular child. The nanny learns what is important to the child's parents in such matters as discipline, educational activi-

---

infant—Imprecise term, but usually refers to a child during the first year of life after which the toddler emerges.

ties, and nutrition. Together, the parents and the nanny can provide the child with consistency and continuity of care.

In-home care provides families with some flexibility in their child-care arrangements. Although nannies work during agreed-upon hours, they can respond to a parent's need for extra or different hours in an emergency or other circumstances. Child-care centers, on the other hand, operate at fixed hours that may not match the hours when a family needs child care.

Parents enjoy peace of mind knowing that while they are away from home, their children are receiving skilled, individualized care in familiar surroundings. Nannies enjoy the satisfaction that comes from giving one-on-one care and knowing they can have a positive influence on a young life. It is not unusual for nannies to form warm and enduring relationships with the families for whom they work and to maintain contact after they are no longer in that particular work situation.

Employment with a private family also has the potential for broadening the nanny's professional and personal experiences in interesting ways. Travel with the employing family in the United States and abroad, opportunities to relocate, and encounters with different cultures and customs are among the advantages that in-home employment situations may offer.

One disadvantage of in-home care is that parents may be concerned that their children will be deprived of the social experiences available in group care. However, children sometimes attend nursery school two or three mornings a week even if they have a nanny. Nannies and their charges can participate in neighborhood play groups. In addition to providing children with opportunities to interact with other children, play groups have the added benefit of reducing the feeling of isolation that a nanny may experience on the job (other ways to cope with isolation are suggested in Chapter Six). Nannies sometimes help to form play groups with other nearby nannies or at-home parents.

When the nanny resides in the employer's home, both the nanny and the family may feel a loss of privacy unless sensible steps are taken to minimize this (see Chapter Four).

A nanny's illness or sudden emergency can create a problem for employers who have to go to work themselves. Employers need to consider this possibility before it happens and have a plan for substitute care.

In-home child care is usually more costly to parents than other forms of care. For the nanny, however, it typically offers much better compensation than employment in a center or family day-care program. When parents employ a nanny, they also have to meet employer responsibilities with respect to taxes and insurance. The nanny should understand the business side of in-home care, too (see Chapter Seven).

THE LARGER EARLY CHILDHOOD COMMUNITY

The rapid increase in the entry of women with children into the labor force during the past 15 years or so has produced an unprecedented need for child care in the United States. According to the U.S. Bureau of Labor Statistics, 38 percent of mothers of children under six years were in the labor force in 1975. By 1993, the rate had risen to nearly 60 percent. In 1975, less than one-third of mothers with infants participated in the labor force. Today, more than one-half of mothers whose youngest child is under two years participate (Figure 1-2). More than five million children under three years are cared for by other adults while parents work. The U.S. Bureau of Labor Statistics projects a 35 percent employment increase in the child day-care services industry between 1988 and 2000.

Early childhood encompasses children from birth through eight years. For working parents of children in this age range, other forms of child care besides in-home care (provided either by a relative or nonrelative) include center-based care and family day care. School-age children are cared for in before- and after-school programs and in vacation programs during the time school is out but parents are at work. Services for children with disabilities or for the child who is mildly ill are among other child-care arrangements that may be available to parents. The federally funded Head Start program was established to target children identified as being at risk of later school failure and pro-

Figure 1.2 With the increase in the number of mothers who work outside the home, quality child care will continue to be an issue and a concern.

vides comprehensive services including early education, health, nutrition, social services, and parent involvement.

Group child care is not a new phenomenon. As America became increasingly industrialized in the latter part of the nineteenth century, day nurseries were established to care for the babies and children of working mothers. More rooted in social welfare than education, day nurseries provided custodial care only. The intent was not to enrich children's lives, but to encourage poor women to work and avoid indigency.

Early childhood education arose from the **kindergarten** movement that originated in Europe in the late nineteenth century. Unlike the day nurseries, kindergarten was child-centered. In the 1920s, early childhood education became established in the

kindergarten—Educational program to prepare young children, usually about age five, for school; term is German for "children's garden."

United States in part-day nursery schools designed to promote the educational and social development of three-, four-, and five-year old children, but not to meet parents' needs for all-day care for children from infancy. Traditionally, care and education have been perceived as separate aspects of childrearing. In modern child care, the two are seen as integrated. The term "early care and education" has come into use recently. It reflects the concept that appropriate practice in the early childhood field provides a safe, nurturing environment that promotes children's physical, social, cognitive, and emotional development while responding to the needs of families.

A growing need for child care in the United States has created challenges for the early childhood community. Ensuring quality of care is a major issue. Currently there are no national requirements for licensing child-care facilities or for certification of child-care practitioners. Regulations are left to local and state governments, resulting in considerable differences in standards. Early childhood and health professionals are calling for improved and uniform standards to assure the best possible care for all children. In 1991, the National Association for the Education of Young Children (NAEYC) established the National Institute for Early Childhood Professional Development. The Institute's purpose is to develop an effective system of professional preparation and career development, key elements in ensuring quality and a strong early childhood profession. NAEYC also administers a national, voluntary accreditation system for early childhood centers and schools.

Nannies have a role to play in ensuring that families have access to child care that suits their needs and preferences. As nannies, they offer the option of in-home child care. As members of the larger early childhood community, they can help shape the future of child care in this country by working on common issues that affect all caregivers and services to children and families. Membership in a professional organization provides opportunities for interaction with caregivers employed in other settings and for contributing the nanny perspective to the field of early childhood (see Appendix D for professional early childhood organizations).

BIBLIOGRAPHY

Bredenkamp, S. (Ed.). (1997). *Developmentally Appropriate Practice in Early Childhood Programs Serving Children from Birth through Age 8*, revised edition. Washington, DC: National Association for the Education of Young Children.

Cable, M. (1975). *The Little Darlings—A History of Child Rearing in America*. New York: Charles Scribner's Sons.

Carnegie Corporation of New York (1994). *Starting Points: Meeting the Needs of Our Youngest Children*—Report of the Carnegie Task Force on Meeting the Needs of Young Children. New York: Carnegie Corporation.

Davis, L.E. (1986). "The Norland Nursery Training College and Its Contribution to the Childcare Profession." Paper delivered at the International Nanny Conference, August 21, 1986, Scripps College, California.

Flating, S. (1991). *Child Care: A Parent's Guide*. New York: Facts on File.

Fyson, N.L. (1977). *Growing Up in the Eighteenth Century*. London, UK: B.T Batford.

Gathorne-Hardy, J. (1973). *The Unnatural History of the Nanny*. New York: The Dial Press.

Giebink, G.S. (1993). "Care of the Ill Child in Day-Care Settings." *Pediatrics* 91(1), 229–233.

Greenleaf, B.K. (1978). *Children Through the Ages: A History of Childhood*. New York: McGraw-Hill.

International Nanny Association (1995). *Directory of Nanny Training Programs, Nanny Placement Agencies and Special Services*, In-Home Child Care Definitions, 3–4. Collingswood, NJ: International Nanny Association.

Library of Congress (1994). *Green Book. Section 12. Child Care*. Source: "Who's Minding the Kids? Child Care Arrangements: Fall 1991." U.S. Department of Commerce, Bureau of the Census, Series P70-36, 1994.

Library of Congress (1994). *Green Book. Section 12. Child Care*. Source: U.S. Department of Labor, Bureau of Labor Statistics.

Miall, A., and Miall, P. (1980). *The Victorian Nursery Book*. New York: Pantheon Books.

Morgan, G. (1991). *Career Progression in Early Care and Education: A Discussion Paper*. Boston: Wheelock College.

National Association for the Education of Young Children (1991): "NAEYC to Launch New Professional Development Initiative." *Young Children* 46(6), 37–39.

O'Conner, S.M. (1995). "Mothering in Public: The Division of Organized Child Care in Kindergarten and the Day Nursery." *Early Childhood Research Quarterly* 10(1), 63–8.

Rice, R. (1987). *The American Nanny*, revised and expanded edition. New York: Harper and Row.

Silvestri, G. (1993). "Wanted: Child Care Workers." *Parents* 68(5), 84.

Stevenson, R.L. (1905). *A Child's Garden of Verses*. New York: Charles Scribner's Sons.

Walsh, P.W., and Brand, L.E. (1990). "Child Day Care Services: An Industry at a Crossroads." *Monthly Labor Review*, December 1990.

Werner, E. (1984). *Child Care: Kith, Kin and Hired Hands*. Baltimore: University Park Press.

Chapter 2

The Role of the Nanny

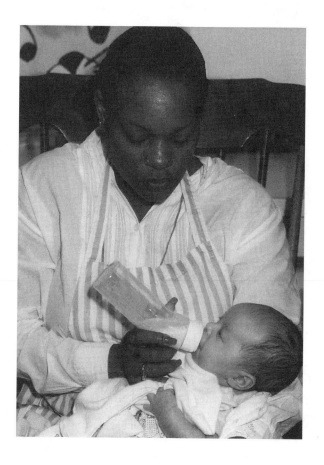

TOPICS

- Introduction
- Nanny/Employer Relationship
- Nanny Responsibilities
- Nanny Qualifications
- Professional Preparation

Terms to Know

status

profession

employment agreement

professional detachment

professionalism

environment

role model

competency

curriculum

hygiene

newborn

personal hygiene

multicultural

ethics

humanities

social sciences

practicum

infant

middle childhood

adolescence

INTRODUCTION

As discussed in Chapter One, the nanny evolved from domestic service. Although nannies traditionally enjoyed higher **status** than members of the domestic staff, there was nevertheless a clear distinction between their social position and that of their employers. In today's society, families who employ nannies are not necessarily of a different social class to the nanny, nor are they always extremely wealthy. Some may employ a full-time housekeeper in addition to a nanny, but a large household staff is rare. Today's employers of nannies are likely to be parents who work hard in their **professions** and who need in-home child care in order to meet the demands of their busy careers while they are raising young children. Unlike Victorian parents, today's mothers and fathers do not want to turn their children's upbringing over to the nanny. They want to be involved in their children's lives and spend time with them. The nanny is often regarded as a team member who works closely with the parents to ensure the well-

---

status—Position or rank, as in society.

*profession—An occupation requiring special preparation and **competencies**.*

being of the children. A nanny can make a big difference in parents' lives as well as the lives of children.

NANNY/EMPLOYER RELATIONSHIP

The working relationship of nannies and their employers is a unique one. Because the employment setting is the home, the line between personal life and professional life is more difficult to draw than in most work situations. The relationship that develops between nannies and employers varies from family to family. In some households, the nanny is included in much of the family's everyday life, such as eating meals together, watching television together in the evening, and other activities. In other households, the nanny and the family lead more separate lives when the nanny is off duty, though meals may be taken together. In a household where the nanny is one of several staff members, the relationship with employers is likely to be impersonal, with little social contact. An understanding of the nanny's position in the household will be reflected in the written **employment agreement** (see Chapter Seven and Appendix A).

In general, nannies become quite closely connected with the parents of the children they care for. The challenge for both parties is to remain friendly while respecting the professional nature of the relationship. A nanny can maintain a more realistic picture of the children and the parents if there is some detachment and if the temptation to "become one of the family" is resisted (**professional detachment** and other aspects of nanny **professionalism** are discussed in Chapter Three). For parents, a close personal relationship with the nanny can make it difficult for them to be effective as employers.

---

employment agreement—*An arrangement between an employer and an employee with respect to the terms of employment.*

professional detachment—*A state of being impartial and impersonal in professional situations.*

professionalism—*A quality of conduct and skills that is worthy of a profession.*

A mutual attitude of respect provides a firm foundation for building a warm but professional relationship from which everyone benefits, particularly the children. To avoid conflict, both the nanny and the employer need to have realistic expectations of the working relationship and know what is necessary to make the relationship a positive one.

As a nanny, there are many steps you can take to make your job personally and professionally satisfying. These are discussed in detail in later chapters of this book. Basic rules to guide the nanny and the employer in developing an effective working relationship may be summarized as follows:

◆ Insist on a personal interview before a job is offered or accepted. It is unrealistic for employers or nannies to think an informed decision can be made without obtaining all relevant information and understanding each other's expectations clearly. This cannot be done by telephone and correspondence alone. An informed decision to come together in a work arrangement is a positive step toward developing a good working relationship.

◆ Agree to a written employment agreement prior to the first day of work. This establishes the responsibilities of both the nanny and employer and is essential for mutual understanding, respect, and communications. A written arrangement puts the relationship on a professional footing where it belongs. It helps to avoid problems and to resolve matters if problems do occur.

◆ The importance of communications cannot be overemphasized. Communications are the foundations of any good relationship. Daily reports and written logs should be part of the nanny's routine, as well as regular meetings with the parents to discuss the children and other matters as they arise. Problems should be addressed promptly and not be allowed to develop into crises.

◆ Agree on a childrearing philosophy. It is unrealistic for nannies or employers to expect to develop a good working relationship if they are not in reasonable agreement about the major issues of childrearing. These need to be discussed before a job is accepted. Nannies should recognize that parents possess the ultimate authority for deciding how their children are to be raised. A nanny who disagrees with a parent's childrearing approaches will not be happy in that working relationship.

◆ Providing the highest quality child care must always be the nanny's priority. Parents may hire the nanny for various reasons, but the most important one is to ensure good care for their children (Figure 2.1). As employers, they have the right to expect that it is the most important aspect of the job for the nanny, too.

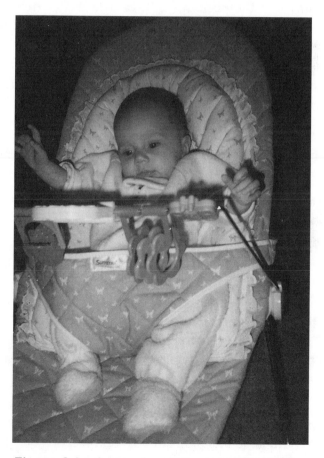

Figure 2.1 A nanny's priority is to provide the highest quality child care.

- ◆ Employers have the right to expect that the nanny will respect their homes and maintain confidentiality about their private affairs.

- ◆ Honoring arrangements for the nanny to have regular time off and recognizing the nanny's need for a personal life is an employer's obligation. Employers cannot expect the nanny to be on call most of the time or to assume responsibility for the entire running of the household.

- ◆ An employer must be prepared to pay a competitive salary, review it regularly, and see that the nanny's paycheck is issued on time.

- ◆ Respect each other's privacy. This is particularly important when the position is a live-in one. Relationships are more likely to flourish when there is physical and psychological breathing space between the parties involved.

- ◆ Finally, remember that all good relationships do not just happen. They require continued nurturing and attention.

Professional relationships are explored further in Chapter Three, aspects of working in a private home in Chapter Four, communications in Chapter Five, employment agreements in Chapter Six, and choosing a nanny position in Chapter Seven.

NANNY RESPONSIBILITIES

As defined by the National Association for the Education of Young Children, early childhood spans the time from birth through eight years. This is the age range with which nannies usually work (in some families there are older children for whom the nanny is expected to provide supervision). A nanny's overall responsibility is to work cooperatively with parents to support the young child's physical, emotional, intellectual, and social development.

Nanny responsibilities can be divided into three broad areas: child-centered responsibilities, domestic responsibilities related to child care, and general nanny employment responsibilities. There is considerable overlap between the three areas and each is important for providing in-home care of the highest quality. Typical nanny responsibilities form the basis for developing a nanny job description and include the following areas.

Child-Centered Responsibilities

- ◆ Promotion of health and safety, including physical care, maintaining a safe, nurturing **environment** and responding appropriately when a child is ill or injured
- ◆ Promotion of security and stability in the child's life
- ◆ Planning and providing a balance of developmentally appropriate activities daily
- ◆ Providing guidance and discipline in accordance with the parent's preferences. Note: Nannies do not use physical punishment and should make this clear to parents before accepting an offer of employment. Some nanny training programs require students to sign a statement that they will not use physical punishment.
- ◆ Planning and providing nutritious meals and snacks for the child
- ◆ Providing a positive **role model** for the child in manners, language, appearance, health and safety

Child-Related Domestic Responsibilities

- ◆ Care of the child's clothing and other personal effects, including laundry, organization and storage, simple repairs and alterations, sewing on name tapes
- ◆ Care and cleaning of child's bedroom/bathroom/playroom
- ◆ Care and cleaning of child's equipment and toys, with attention to safety maintenance

---

environment—*Physical, cultural, and behavioral conditions that surround and influence an individual.*

role model—*A person whose behavior serves as an example to others and inspires them to copy the behavior.*

- Food preparation and clean-up for the child
- Child-related errands, shopping, and transportation

General Nanny Employment Responsibilities

- In a full-time position, providing child care 8 to 12 hours a day, five days a week
- Regular communications with parents, including keeping a daily log
- Cooperation with other professionals involved in promoting the child's well-being, such as teachers, physicians, nurses, dentists
- In a live-in position, care of the nanny's accommodations
- Commitment to continued education and professional development as a nanny
- Facilitating an effective working relationship with the employer and other members of the household (Figure 2.2)

Figure 2.2   Regular communications with parents, including keeping a daily log, is an important nanny responsibility.

Additional Responsibilities

Depending on the particular employment situation, a nanny may agree to undertake additional responsibilities such as:

◆ Travel with the family.

◆ Assisting with family entertaining.

◆ Supervision of other household staff; arranging for household repairs.

◆ Additional child-care coverage or occasional 24-hour duty when parents are away.

◆ Care of pets during the employer's absence.

NANNY QUALIFICATIONS

In order to fulfill the responsibilities of a nanny, certain skills and knowledge, or nanny **competencies**, are required. Many of these competencies are necessary to care for young children regardless of where care is given. Others are necessary because of the particular setting in which nannies apply their child-care skills, that is, the private home.

As a career option in the field of early care and education, becoming a professional nanny is relatively new in the United States and national standards for nanny training and practice have yet to be established. The International Nanny Association (INA) has developed recommended competencies for the education of nannies. They include competencies related to: meeting the developmental needs of children, the physical care of children, domestic tasks and care of the child's environment, interaction with parents/employers, family dynamics, and personal development and social skills.

In the larger early childhood community, the National Association for the Education of Young Children (NAEYC) is in the process of developing a system of early childhood professional development to ensure well-qualified practitioners and promote career advancement. As part of this process, NAEYC has identified some common areas of skills and knowledge in which all early

---

competency—Demonstrable skill and knowledge.

childhood professionals should be competent. These include: child development; observation and assessment of children's behavior; safe and healthy environments; developmentally appropriate **curriculum**; guidance techniques; relationships with families; professionalism; and family, society and culture.

Keeping in mind nanny responsibilities and the areas of competency for caregivers suggested by INA and NAEYC, the following checklist provides guidelines for what a nanny needs to know and be able to link to competent performance.

Child Development

- ◆ Ages and stages of development, prenatal to eight years
- ◆ Observation and assessment of children's behavior
- ◆ Consistent daily routines for children
- ◆ Appropriate guidance techniques for various ages
- ◆ Early childhood curriculum
- ◆ Adult role in supporting children's play
- ◆ Selection, organization, and maintenance of age-appropriate play materials and equipment
- ◆ Outings for children
- ◆ Developing children's language skills
- ◆ Adult role in supporting children's social and emotional development
- ◆ Identification of emotional problems
- ◆ Appropriate adjustments for children with special needs

Physical Care

- ◆ Relationship of physical care and overall development
- ◆ Nursery **hygiene**, safety, and comfort
- ◆ Selection and care of layette and nursery equipment

---

curriculum—A plan for learning.

hygiene—The study of health and the practice of measures to promote and maintain health.

- **Newborn** care
- Infant feeding (including bottle preparation, care of feeding equipment, and support of the breastfeeding mother)
- Healthy routines for infants/children
- **Personal hygiene** for infants/children
- Toilet training approaches
- Selection and care of children's clothing and footwear
- Nutritious meals and snacks for children
- Cultural and religious influences on food choices
- Maintenance of children's bedroom, bathroom, playroom, and equipment
- Care for infant/child at any period during 24 hours
- Management of injuries and emergencies, including first aid and cardiopulmonary resuscitation (CPR)
- Recognition of common illnesses and appropriate action for the caregiver to take
- Care of the mildly ill child
- Infection control, hygienic practices
- Accurate record keeping
- Coordination of health promotion with parents and health professionals
- Care of children while traveling
- Health education for children

Safe Environments

- Common dangers to children at each age and stage
- Principles of accident prevention
- Safety precautions in a private home (indoors and outside)
- Safety precautions in the community

---

newborn—*The infant during the first four weeks after birth. Also called a neonate.*

personal hygiene—*Personal habits contributing to health, such as handwashing, bathing/showering, care of teeth, nails and hair, and wearing clean clothes.*

- ◆ Car safety, defensive driving
- ◆ Water safety
- ◆ Home security, household emergencies
- ◆ Self-defense and personal safety
- ◆ Drug abuse
- ◆ Safety education for children

Family Relationships

- ◆ The family in society
- ◆ Patterns of family life today
- ◆ **Multicultural** awareness
- ◆ Social and cultural adjustments
- ◆ Positive interactions between nanny/child/family
- ◆ Loss and grief
- ◆ Domestic violence
- ◆ Child protection (abuse and neglect)
- ◆ Community resources serving families

Professionalism

- ◆ **Ethics** in child care
- ◆ Principles of confidentiality
- ◆ Employment options for nannies
- ◆ Résumé and portfolio preparation
- ◆ Process of obtaining employment
- ◆ Employer/employee responsibilities
- ◆ Terms of employment
- ◆ Nanny employment agreement

---

multicultural—*Culturally diverse; coming from various different cultures.*

ethics—*Code of conduct of a particular person, profession, religion, or other group.*

- Time management and priority setting
- Carrying out instructions accurately
- Accurate record keeping
- Personal health and development
- Professional appearance
- Social skills
- Continued education
- Resources for nannies

Homemaking Skills

- Cleaning and sanitation methods
- Food purchasing and preparation
- Use of appliances
- Kitchen hygiene
- Wise consumerism
- Laundry methods, ironing
- Care of footwear
- Sewing skills

Resources and books relevant to nanny competencies are suggested in Appendices D and E.

General Knowledge and Additional Skills

General knowledge of the liberal arts form the basis for developing early childhood curriculum, as well as broadening the nanny's understanding and appreciation of the world. Knowledge of the creative arts, **humanities**, science, mathematics, and the **social sciences** enhances the nanny's professional and per-

---

humanities—Fields of learning concerned with human thought and relationships, such as literature, philosophy, history, and languages.

social sciences—*The study of people in society in such fields as sociology, psychology, political science, and economics.*

sonal skills. Other subjects of value include physical education, computer skills, foreign languages, and the performing arts.

Since a nanny's responsibilities usually include child-related errands and transportation, the possession of a valid driver's license and a good driving record are considered to be necessary qualifications for a nanny, with rare exceptions.

Personal Characteristics

Taking into consideration the responsibilities nannies undertake and the position of trust that they hold, certain personal characteristics seem to be desirable for success as a nanny. Based on experience rather than scientific study, nanny employers, placement agencies, and training programs repeatedly mention several personal characteristics as being important for a nanny's success.

First and foremost, a nanny must have deep appreciation and respect for children. A nanny must truly like working with children and families and recognize that the job, as any job, will sometimes be tedious or difficult as well as rewarding. Entering the field of in-home child care with an unrealistic notion of what it means to care for young children or because the job seems to offer opportunities to associate with the rich and famous is bound to lead to disappointment.

Trustworthiness is high on the list of desirable nanny characteristics. An employer must be able to have confidence that the nanny always carries out responsibilities conscientiously and is always honest with them. The employer must be able to rely on the nanny's discretion with respect to family and business affairs. They must be certain that the nanny will not abuse the privileges of their home when they are away.

Independence is necessary for success as a nanny. This includes possessing a good sense of self and accepting responsibility for handling one's own life. A nanny must be able to manage personal finances, maintain a healthy lifestyle, and develop friendships and interests beyond work without relying on someone else's help or urging.

A nanny needs to possess a good deal of common sense and resourcefulness to deal calmly and effectively with emergencies. The different needs and situations that a nanny will encounter require flexibility and a willingness to adjust.

A nanny must be assertive enough to be able to negotiate a satisfactory work arrangement with employers and to address conflicts constructively and with equanimity as they arise.

For positive relationships with children and parents, a cheerful disposition and a sense of humor are indispensable. Although child care is serious, responsible work, a nanny needs to have a sense of fun and the ability to play.

Good health and stamina are essential for work with young children. A nanny must be an active person and fit to meet the physical and emotional demands of child care. Families commonly stipulate that the nanny must be a non-smoker.

PROFESSIONAL PREPARATION

The purpose of professional preparation is to provide educational experiences that are likely to develop the competencies needed to carry out professional responsibilities (Figure 2.3). In the United States, nanny training programs have been available in community colleges, private colleges, private career schools, and vocational/technical schools since 1983. Programs come in a variety of models.

Community colleges typically offer a one-year certificate program, with the option to complete a second year for an associate degree. Nanny programs usually include coursework required of all early childhood students and cover orientation to early education and care, child development, observation and assessment of children's behavior, guidance and discipline, health and safety, nutrition, creative activities, family relationships, and supervised **practicum** in group settings.

---

practicum—A course in which a student gains practical experience in a field of study.

Figure 2.3   The need for quality in-home child care has led to the establishment of nanny training programs in the United States.
(Courtesy Murray State College, Tishomingo, Oklahoma)

Nanny programs also include preparation in additional skills and knowledge needed for specializing in in-home child care. This preparation typically includes nanny professionalism and personal development, practical **infant** and child-care skills, homemaking skills, home nursing skills, safety and security at home and while traveling, communications, and social skills. Because nannies sometimes supervise older children, **middle childhood** and **adolescence** may be covered in child development in addition to early childhood. Tutoring skills may also be covered. Human development across the life span may be part of a nanny program to increase the nanny's self-awareness and to prepare for working with different generations in the family setting. Psychology, sociology, and special education are among the other

---

infant—Imprecise term, but usually refers to a child during the first year of life, after which the toddler emerges.

*middle childhood—Stage of development between preschool and **adolescence**, from about six to twelve years of age.*

adolescence—Period of human development between onset of puberty (sexual maturity) and the beginning of adulthood.

subjects that may be included in a nanny program. Two-year associate degree nanny programs include general education requirements. In addition to supervised practicum in group settings, some nanny programs include supervised experience with hospitalized children or with children in private homes.

BIBLIOGRAPHY

Breese, C. and Gomer, H. (1988). *The Good Nanny Guide*. London: Century Hutchinson, Ltd.

Davis, L.E. (1988). "The Nanny as a Professional Child-Care Worker." Paper delivered at the 1988 Distinguished Visiting Scholar Program: The American Nanny Comes of Age, California State University at Los Angeles, April 1988.

Davis, L.E. (1987). "Nannies and Parents: A Unique Working Relationship." *Our Children Are Our Future* (booklet for parents). Honolulu, HI: Honolulu Community College.

Forney, D. (1985). "What Qualities Make a Successful Nanny?" *National Nanny Newsletter* 1 (5), 9.

International Nanny Association. (1995). *Directory of Nanny Training Programs, Nanny Placement Agencies, and Special Services*. Collingswood, NJ: International Nanny Association.

International Nanny Association (1989). *Recommended Competencies for the Education of Nannies* (information sheet). Collingswood, NJ: International Nanny Association.

National Association for the Education of Young Children (1994). "NAEYC Position Statement: A Conceptual Framework for Early Childhood Professional Development." *Young Children* 49(3), 68–77.

National Nursery Examination Board (1993). *Diploma and Preliminary Diploma in Nursery Nursing: Modular Scheme Overview 1993/94*. St. Albans, UK: National Nursery Examination Board.

Readdick, C. (1987). "Schools for the American Nanny: Training In-Home Child Care Specialists." *Young Children* 42(4), 72–79.

Chapter 3

Professionalism for the Nanny

TOPICS

- Introduction
- Professional Ethics
- Commitment to Children
- Child Advocacy
- Integrity
- Confidentiality
- Recognizing Your Limitations

- Continued Education
- Professional Relationships with Employers
- Professional Appearance and Demeanor
- Professional Detachment
- Relationships with Other Professionals

Terms to Know

colleague

professionalism

ethics

dignity

socioeconomic

ethnic

advocate

integrity

unethical

lifestyle

belief

value

personal hygiene

demeanor

self-respect

professional detachment

objectively

bias

INTRODUCTION

This chapter is designed to help you consider how to present yourself in your role as a nanny and how to build professional relationships with children, families, **colleagues** and the general public.

Professionalism for the nanny encompasses more than the special hands-on skills needed to take care of children. It includes the underlying knowledge and understanding behind the techniques you use, knowledge of self, acceptance of others, and the development of habits of behavior that enable you to be an effective nanny. A professional approach is also likely to lead to satisfaction in your chosen field of work. It makes the work you are doing an art rather than a task-oriented job.

Professional behavior is an essential part of nanny practice. This chapter examines professional expectations for nannies and what these mean in the everyday work situation.

---

colleague—Person of the same profession.

professionalism—A quality of conduct and skills that is worthy of a profession.

PROFESSIONAL ETHICS

Ethics are rules about fitting and proper conduct. The rules may be written or unwritten. When ethics guide the individual's actions, they produce ethical behavior. The responsibility for deciding whether to behave in an ethical manner rests with the individual.

An organized group very often has a written code of conduct with which members are expected to comply in the course of their work. The code of conduct helps the group to carry out its purpose, serve the best interests of its clients and earn the public trust.

Fundamentally, ethics have to do with how we perceive and treat other people. Those in the caring professions, such as early care and education, have a special obligation to value and uphold the **dignity** of every person regardless of age, **socioeconomic** status, **ethnic** origin, race, gender, marital status, religion, or disability. When working with young children, it is especially important to respect their rights and meet their needs because children are usually unable to speak for themselves adequately.

Based on its code of ethical conduct, the National Association for the Education of Young Children has developed a statement of commitment for its members (see Figure 3.1). Similarly, the International Nanny Association has recommended practices for its member nannies (see Figure 3.2). Notice how the basic principles underlying rules of ethical conduct for all who work with young children include obligations to children, to families/employers, to colleagues, to society, and to self.

---

ethics—Code of conduct of a particular person, profession, religion, or other group.

dignity—Sense of proper pride in who one is and what one does.

socioeconomic—Involving both social and economic factors.

ethnic—Pertaining to a group of people distinguished by a common history, customs, language, and other shared characteristics.

Statement of Commitment

As an individual who works with young children, I commit myself to furthering the values of early childhood education as they are reflected in the NAEYC Code of Ethical Conduct.

To the best of my ability I will

◆ Ensure that programs for young children are based on current knowledge of child development and early childhood education.

◆ Respect and support families in their task of nurturing children.

◆ Respect colleagues in early childhood education and support them in maintaining the NAEYC Code of Ethical Conduct.

◆ Serve as an advocate for children, their families, and their teachers in community and society.

◆ Maintain high standards of professional conduct.

◆ Recognize how personal values, opinions, and biases can affect professional judgment.

◆ Be open to new ideas and be willing to learn from the suggestions of others.

◆ Continue to learn, grow, and contribute as a professional.

◆ Honor the ideals and principles of the NAEYC Code of Ethical Conduct.

The Statement of Commitment expresses those basic personal commitments that individuals must make in order to align themselves with the profession's responsibilities as set forth in the NAEYC Code of Ethical Conduct.

Figure 3.1   Reprinted with permission from the publisher, Statement of Commitment from Code of Ethical Conduct & Statement of Commitment: *Guidelines for Responsible Behavior in Early Childhood* by S. Feeney and K. Kipnis (Washington, DC: National Association for the Education of Young Children, 1992). © by NAEYC.

Recommended Practices for Nannies

To promote quality child care and an environment for all children that nurtures their well-being, the International Nanny Association recommends the following practices for nannies.

Professionalism

Participate in personal and professional growth activities.

INA recommends that nannies become involved in social, cultural and educational activities not only to maintain and improve their child-care skills, but also to enhance their own personal growth. Suggested activities include professional development classes, seminars and training programs, participation in career-related professional organizations, and involvement in community affairs.

Act as an advocate for young children.

INA recommends that nannies promote knowledge and understanding of young children and their needs and rights. Nannies should be familiar with the signs of child abuse and neglect and be knowledgeable of procedures for dealing with them.

Review INA professional practices.

INA recommends that before accepting a new assignment a nanny review these practices. INA has no authority to require a member to adhere to them and cannot discipline a member who does not abide by the letter or spirit of what is recommended. Consequently, INA assumes no responsibility of liability for the action of any member.

Relationships with Children

Respect each child as a unique individual.

INA recommends that nannies recognize the individuality of the child/children in their care by creating an environment that fosters trust, self-esteem, and independence in children, and by using consistent daily routines and developmentally appropriate behavior management techniques.

Provide developmentally appropriate play and learning experiences.

INA recommends that nannies provide for the physical, emotional, intellectual, and social needs of children by using developmentally appropriate play/learning activities, materials, and equipment.

Create and maintain a safe and healthy environment for children.

INA recommends that nannies promote the physical and emotional well-being of children by serving nutritious meals and snacks; supervising

(Continues)

Figure 3.2 Recommended Practices for Nannies.
(Reprinted with permission of International Nanny Association)

INA Commitment to Professional Excellence

- Respect the contributions of individuals and organizations involved in professional in-home child care.
- Maintain high standards of professional conduct.
- Respect and support families in their task of nurturing children.
- Promote the physical, emotional, intellectual, and social development of children.
- Support the lifelong process of personal growth and professional development.

In recognition of their responsibilities to children and families, members of the International Nanny Association make these commitments in support of professional in-home child care.

rest periods, naps, and sleep; recognizing symptoms of common childhood illnesses; handling emergency situations; administering first aid; teaching children the hygienic way to bathe and wash hands, hair, and teeth; taking every safety precaution when traveling with children; performing domestic tasks related to the care and maintenance of the child's areas of the home such as bedroom, playroom, bathroom, and outside play space; laundering and making simple repairs to children's clothing; and observing safety rules in the home.

Communicate effectively at the child's level of understanding.

INA recommends that nannies model appropriate language for children, recognize stages of language development in children, and engage in activities that encourage language development.

Relationships with Parents/Employers

Request a personal interview with prospective employers.

INA recommends that nannies interview prospective employers in person, preferably in the family's home.

Request a descriptive, written work agreement detailing conditions of employment.

INA recommends that, at a minimum, a work agreement include the following: job duties, hours and days of duty, salary amount, when and how paid and compensation for overtime worked, employer's legally required tax obligations, fringe benefits such as health insurance, holiday and vacation policies, sick leave if offered, probationary period, frequency of work agreement review, terms of notice of termination, and grounds for dismissal.

Figure 3.2   *Continued*

Respect the family's right to privacy.

INA recommends that nannies show good judgment in maintaining confidentiality about the private lives of the families for whom they work.

Support the childrearing philosophy of the employer.

INA recommends that nannies recognize the ultimate authority of parents in making decisions about the welfare and care of their child/children by respecting the parent/employer's philosophy of child rearing.

Develop positive relationships with the family.

INA recommends that nannies work cooperatively with the family, perform duties as agreed, communicate openly and effectively, show sensitivity to family situations, seek constructive solutions of problems, and maintain a consistent, positive attitude.

Relationships with Agencies

Be clear about placement agency services and required fees prior to using agency services.

INA recommends that nannies obtain a full and complete explanation of agency services, expectations, requirements, and fees before becoming obligated to an agency.

Accurately and truthfully represent personal job qualifications and experience.

INA recommends that nannies provide complete, accurate, and truthful information about their background, education, special skills and abilities, and prior work experience.

Request descriptive information about prospective employers.

INA recommends that in addition to details about a particular position such as working hours, working conditions, salary and benefits, nannies also obtain all information available about the employing family. A placement agency can provide details about family needs and preferences and may also be able to supply the names and phone numbers of family references whom the nanny can contact of desired.

> *The international Nanny Association recommends these practices, but has no authority to require a member to adhere to them. INA does not represent that the Association has the authority to discipline a member for the violation of the letter or spirit of what is recommended. Consequently, INA assumes no responsibility or liability for the action of any member of the Association.*

Figure 3.2 *Continued*

Ethics are the foundation of professional behavior. Each nanny has the responsibility to know and abide by the guidelines that help those in early care and education meet their obligations.

COMMITMENT TO CHILDREN

The paramount concern of a nanny is to promote the well-being of children. This includes not only contributing in positive ways to children's lives, but also to the lives of their families.

Child-care practices must be based on the latest knowledge of child development and current recommendations for keeping children safe and healthy. Ways to assure appropriate practice include joining a professional early childhood organization, reading reports of recent research in journals, attending professional workshops or taking courses to improve your skills, and following the advice of the child's own physician and dentist.

A nanny values each child as an individual. Recognizing that each child is unique, a nanny plans and provides care according to the child's individual capabilities and needs. Together with parents, teachers, and others involved with the child, a nanny provides experiences to help the child reach his or her potential. For some children, this may mean supporting a special talent or hobby. For others, it may mean working on an area of developmental delay or difficulty where extra help is needed. This individual approach includes a willingness to try different techniques with different children, because what works for one may not work for another. For example, discipline, toilet training, or techniques for settling down at bedtime will vary from child to child. Each child in a nanny's care must be treated with respect and patience (Figure 3.3).

Keeping children safe and secure is fundamental to good child care. A nanny maintains an environment that promotes the child's physical and psychological well-being. Circumstances that may jeopardize a child's health or safety cannot be ignored. A nanny must become familiar with child protection laws and know what to do if there is reason to suspect that a child is being abused or neglected (see Chapter Eleven).

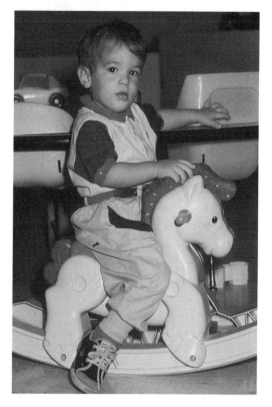

Figure 3.3 A nanny values each child as an individual.

CHILD ADVOCACY

An **advocate** is someone who speaks and acts on behalf of someone else. Children need caring adults to speak for them to bring about changes that will improve their lives. As individual child-care practitioners and as members of the wider early childhood profession, nannies can and should be advocates for children—not only for the children in their care, but for children in general. Children cannot vote and influence legislation that affects their lives. Make sure you are registered to vote in whichever community you live, and exercise your voting privi-

---

advocate—*One who speaks or acts in support of another's cause.*

lege. Nannies should be aware of who their elected officials are at the local, state, and federal levels and how they stand on issues concerning children and families. Membership in a professional early childhood organization is an effective way to keep informed about child-related issues and advocate on behalf of children. Nannies need to be aware of situations in their local communities that affect children's health, safety, education, or any other aspect of well-being. For example, there may be a neighborhood hazard that threatens children's safety, or a school tax on the ballot, or a program that is needed to serve a particular group of children. A nanny can demonstrate professional commitment by becoming informed and involved.

INTEGRITY

Integrity is a quality of honesty and moral principle that runs through and through the person who possesses it and is evident in everyday life as well as at work.

Given the position of great trust that nannies occupy, integrity is an essential component of their professional behavior. Professional relationships are built on trust. Once that trust is broken, the relationship and the effectiveness of the professional are damaged, often beyond repair.

Parents have to have absolute confidence in your integrity when they leave you in charge of their children and home. A nanny often works without supervision. Parents have to trust the nanny to adhere to the highest standards of practice regardless of whether they or anyone else is watching. Other examples of integrity include truthfulness about qualifications and experiences when seeking a nanny position, keeping commitments even when it is inconvenient to do so, providing parents with complete and accurate daily reports, and not making promises to children that cannot be kept. It includes respecting the employers' home, property, and any house policies they have established whether they are away or present. Integrity is an obligation nannies owe not only to themselves, employers, and children, but to the profession.

---

integrity—Quality of uncompromising honesty and moral principle.

CONFIDENTIALITY

Confidentiality is another essential component of the trust relationship you want to build with your employers. A nanny owes employers the obligation not to reveal confidential information without their express permission, except when disclosure is required by law, by the court, or to protect a child's well-being. In this event, information must still be handled discreetly and only given to the appropriate authorities (see Chapter Eleven).

When the employment setting is a private home, there are many opportunities to become aware of the employers' business and household affairs, as well as their habits and other personal details of their everyday lives. Nannies also learn a great deal about the children in their care. Maintaining confidentiality is expected in any professional relationship and it is considered **unethical** to reveal private matters about a client. Careless talk on the part of a nanny also has the potential to jeopardize the security of the home and the safety of the children. Remember that once information is shared with someone else, you have no control over where it goes next.

Confidentiality begins even before a position is accepted. During the interview process, information about potential employers must be handled with discretion. When a nanny leaves a position, confidentiality concerning former employers must be maintained. Confidentiality also extends to respecting the privacy of colleagues and co-workers.

RECOGNIZING YOUR LIMITATIONS

A mark of professionals is to know not only what their responsibilities are, but also to recognize and acknowledge the limitations of their area of expertise and competence. You may have to decline to undertake a function or task for which you have not been prepared until you receive instruction and gain competency. For example, you may need training in a home nursing

---

unethical—Not conforming to an expected code of conduct or moral standards.

procedure that a child needs but with which you have no experience. Alternatively, some functions and tasks may be more appropriately referred to someone else with the necessary expertise and competence. For example, if you suspect a child is delayed in language development, you should assist the parents in arranging for the child to be further assessed by the appropriate professional. Or, unless you are a certified lifeguard, you should not undertake to supervise children at a swimming pool or beach in the absence of their parents or a lifeguard. In order to serve the best interests of children and families, nannies do not assume responsibilities for which they are not qualified.

CONTINUED EDUCATION

Professionals do not stop learning at the completion of their initial training. They know that in order to provide the best possible services to their clients, they must continually reinforce and update their skills and knowledge. Child development and health, both of which concern the early childhood profession, are rapidly changing fields. It is very important for the nanny to practice according to recommendations based on the latest research.

Membership in a professional early childhood organization gives nannies access to publications, workshops, and conferences. Attending a professional workshop or conference also provides opportunities to share ideas and experiences with others in the field of early childhood. Taking a course relevant to early care and education at a local community college is another way to continue education while working as a nanny.

Nannies have a responsibility to be trained in first aid and cardiopulmonary resuscitation so they can respond appropriately to a child's emergency injury or illness. It is important to maintain these skills by signing up promptly for a course when your certificate is due to expire. The nanny should also consider training in water or boat safety, or lifeguard certification.

Developing a personal resource library is yet another way to maintain and improve professional skills. Not only can you refer to the books, journals, and other publications that you collect, but you can share them with your employers to help assure consistent, developmentally appropriate child care. A list of books is suggested in Appendix E. Other resources for nannies concerning continued education are found in Appendix D.

PROFESSIONAL RELATIONSHIPS WITH EMPLOYERS

Parents, like their children, are unique individuals whose human dignity a nanny is professionally bound to uphold. They may have a cultural or religious background that differs from the one in which the nanny grew up. Their **lifestyle** may differ from the nanny's. Such differences must be respected and the nanny must take care not to impose personal **beliefs** and **values** on the employing family (influences on family life and upbringing are discussed in Chapter Four).

Although the nanny's employment setting is a private home, it is important to remember that it is the work place and the relationship with the parents is a professional one. The personal life of a nanny should be kept separate from professional life. In any employment situation, there are limits that should not be exceeded with respect to sharing personal information with a supervisor or employer, and the nanny situation is no exception. It is unprofessional to use an employer as a confidante in the way a friend or relative might be used. Unresolved problems from the nanny's own childhood and family relationships can sometimes interfere with establishing a professional relationship with employers. Employers do not want a nanny who treats them as substitute parents or family. They want a nanny who is mature and independent.

---

lifestyle—A person's way of life, exemplified by his or her possessions, activities, attitudes, and manner.

belief—Acceptance that certain things are true.

value—A social principle or standard held or accepted by an individual, class, or society.

While on duty, it is inconsistent with professional behavior for the nanny to socialize with friends, make or receive personal telephone calls, drink alcoholic beverages, or smoke. A nanny must never abuse the privileges that result from working in a private home whether on duty or off.

Employers expect punctuality and regular attendance, but the nanny must also arrive on duty rested, nourished, and ready to work. A nanny needs to maintain physical and emotional health in order to meet responsibilities in the best way possible.

Again, it needs to be emphasized that trust is the basis for professional relationships and the nanny must be a person in whom employers can have complete confidence.

PROFESSIONAL APPEARANCE AND DEMEANOR

Another way in which a nanny inspires confidence and shows professionalism is by attention to attire, **personal hygiene** and grooming, good manners, and appropriate behavior in general. Imagine how reluctant travelers would be to board an airplane if the crew reported for duty looking slovenly and unkempt, or how patients would be put off by a physician who was rude or silly. When we entrust our well-being to various kinds of professionals, their outer appearance and **demeanor** make an impression on us. Nannies, too, must be aware of the impression they make, for themselves and for the early childhood profession of which they are a part. Nannies also have a responsibility to set a good example for children.

Most American families do not require the nanny to wear a uniform. Parents may be concerned that their children's safety could be compromised if it is obvious they employ a nanny, or they may just prefer the nanny to blend in with the family.

---

personal hygiene—*Personal habits contributing to health, such as handwashing, bathing/showering, care of teeth, nails and hair, and wearing clean clothes.*

demeanor—*Way of conducting oneself.*

Whether or not a uniform is worn, nannies can demonstrate pride in themselves and the work that they do by their appearance (see Chapter Six for dress, grooming, and wardrobe planning).

Courtesy and dignity are characteristics of professional demeanor. Respect for other human beings is demonstrated through kindness and consideration. Furthermore, the nanny needs to provide children with a positive role model for how people should be treated. The saying that "good manners are caught, not taught" is worth remembering. Dignity implies behavior that is consistent with the nanny's responsibilities and with **self-respect**. It is certainly within the bounds of professional behavior to have fun with children—indeed, it is difficult to imagine anyone who truly appreciates children and childhood not having fun—but the nanny must never forget that contributing to the healthy development of the next generation is serious work.

PROFESSIONAL DETACHMENT

The ability to step back from a situation, look at it **objectively**, and use reason to solve problems is essential for professional success. This ability, referred to as **professional detachment**, enables the nanny to make work-related decisions based on professional knowledge and ethics rather than personal beliefs and **biases**. All individuals are influenced by upbringing and other experiences to form opinions, accept certain things as true, and develop preconceived notions about things. In professional life, such beliefs and biases can interfere with doing what is best for the client. When faced with a problem, the nanny should seek the solution most consistent with promoting the child's well-being. The way to

---

self-respect—Proper respect for one's worth as a person.

objectively—Describes unprejudiced, detached perception that is independent of one's own subjective thoughts and feelings.

professional detachment—A state of being impartial and impersonal in professional situations.

bias—Prejudice or inclination toward a particular point of view.

resolve a work-related problem may not be the way you would choose if the problem affected you personally.

Professional detachment can strengthen the nanny/employer relationship. For example, the nanny understands when an employer, tired from a difficult day at work, is short-tempered with the nanny. Rather than take it personally, the nanny looks for a creative solution to ease the employer's situation. Instead of an angry reaction, the nanny uses a thoughtful, rational approach so everyone benefits, including the children.

Those in the caring professions do feel for their clients' joys and sorrows, but they are careful to distinguish between the kind of involvement they would have with their own families and what is appropriate in a professional relationship. Without professional detachment, professional judgment and effectiveness are reduced. When you work as a nanny in the intimacy of a private home, you are close to much of what happens in the family. It is important to achieve a balance between establishing a warm and pleasant relationship with children, their parents, and other relatives and maintaining your professional detachment (see Chapter Four for further discussion of the private home as the work setting).

RELATIONSHIPS WITH OTHER PROFESSIONALS

Professionals treat each other with courtesy and respect. Another part of a nanny's obligation is to cooperate with other professionals whose work focuses on the well-being of children and their families. It is not unusual for the nanny to have contact with physicians, nurses, dentists and other health professionals, teachers and others in early care and education, social workers, and other related professionals. The nanny has a particular contribution to make to children, families, and society, but must also acknowledge the contributions of others and be willing to work as part of a team. Furthermore, it is well to remember that other professionals will form opinions about nannies in general from their encounters with the individual nanny.

There are many ways in which nannies can work cooperatively with other professionals and present a positive image for all nannies. Your individual circumstances will determine how you do this. There will almost certainly be opportunities to show cooperation with the child's physician and dentist by communicating with them appropriately and following their instructions. If the child in your care has some special need, you may be involved in carrying out home therapy as directed by the professional concerned. Support for the child's teachers can be shown by seeing that homework or music practice gets done. In the event you suspect the child or family has a problem beyond the scope of your skill and knowledge, you should suggest an appropriate source of professional help. Nannies need to become familiar with services and programs for children and families in their communities (see Appendix F).

BIBLIOGRAPHY

Counselman, K. (1987). "What is Your Professional Quotient (PQ)?" *National Nanny Newsletter* 3(4), 5.

Feeney, S., and Kipnis, K. (1992). *Code of Ethical Conduct: Guidelines for Behavior in Early Childhood Education* (brochure). Washington, DC: National Association for the Education of Young Children.

Feeney, S., and Kipnis, K. (1985). "Professional Ethics in Early Childhood Education." *Young Children* 40(3), 54–56.

International Nanny Association (1995). *Recommended Practices for Nannies* (information sheet). Collingswood, NJ: International Nanny Association.

Katz, L.G., and Ward, E. (1978). *Ethical Behavior in Early Childhood.* Washington, DC: National Association for the Education of Young Children.

National Association for the Education of Young Children (1994). "Using NAEYC's Code of Ethics: A Tool for Real Life." *Young Children* 49(5), 56–57.

National Nursery Examination Board (1990). *Principles of Professional Practice.* St. Albans, UK: National Nursery Examination Board.

Rodomski, M.A. (1986). "Professionalization of Early Childhood Educators." *Young Children* 41(5), 20–23.

Chapter 4

The Private Home as the Work Setting

TOPICS

- ◆ Introduction
- ◆ The Family in Society
- ◆ The Influence of Culture, Religion, and Social Class on Family Life
- ◆ Parenting Styles and Situations

- ◆ Divorce
- ◆ Death in the Family
- ◆ Nanny/Child/Parent Relationships

Terms to Know

cohabitation

socialization

status

egalitarian

industrialization

suffrage

authoritarian

culture

social class

custom

sex role

value

belief

bias

ethnic

ritual

lifestyle

discipline

permissive

authoritative

autonomy

attachment

postpartum

baby blues

extended family

grief

regressive behavior

custody

INTRODUCTION

In-home child care clearly has the potential for a productive partnership between the nanny and the parents. They share the goal of promoting the child's healthy development. They each have knowledge and skills to contribute to the partnership. The home, in which the nanny and the parents work for the child's well-being, is the natural environment for childrearing. This chapter examines family life and the nanny's role in supporting parents in their all-important task of childrearing.

THE FAMILY IN SOCIETY

Most of us know what a family is through the experience of being a member of a particular family. Understanding families in general begins by considering what a family is and its significance to society.

Definitions and Functions of the Family

For the 1990 census, the United States Bureau of the Census defined a family as a householder and one or more persons living in the same household related to the householder by birth, marriage, or adoption. All persons in a household who are related to the householder are considered to be members of his or her family. For purposes of the census, one person is designated as the householder and in most cases, this is the person, or one of the persons, in whose name the home is owned or rented. This definition does not take into account household arrangements such as **cohabitation**, gay marriages, communes, or persons living alone.

The family can also be defined as one of the basic social institutions in society, together with political, economic, educational, and religious institutions. Social institutions perform functions necessary to meet the needs of a society and ensure its survival.

The family serves society in several important ways, such as giving birth to new members of the society, a task essential to the continuation of the society. The family has the basic responsibility for the care and **socialization** of new members while they are young. Through socialization, children acquire the attitudes, skills, discipline, tastes, and aspirations that enable them to participate in family life, and, gradually, in the life of the larger community. The family also serves as an agent for transmitting property from one generation to another. It is the basic social unit of economic cooperation. On an individual level, the family satisfies the emotional and sexual needs of marriage partners. The need for love and affection is largely met through parent/child and husband/wife relationships.

American Families Past

From past to present, family life has been shaped by social conditions and events. In order to understand the family of today, one needs to know something of the family of the past and how it has changed over time.

---

cohabitation—*Living together as though married when not legally married.*

socialization—*The process of learning to become an acceptable member of the society in which one lives.*

Work and family were closely intertwined in colonial America where most people were farmers or involved in a family business. Women and children were valued for their economic contributions to the family as workers. However, a wife's property belonged to her husband and she had no legal claim to her children. The family performed many functions, such as children's education and the care of the sick, the elderly, and the orphaned. Family life was also closely tied to the community, which took an active part in regulating behavior within the family. As in Europe, children often served as apprentices in the homes of other families. There was little concept of childhood as we understand it now. Parents considered it their duty to bring their children up strictly.

Society felt the effects of conditions in the New World. Population grew and became more diverse. Free land enabled individuals and families to leave the constraints of tightly knit communities. Family ties were weakened. Although men remained the authority in the family, frontier life produced resourceful women who faced dangers and challenges equally with men. Women were scarce on the frontier—this also improved their **status**. Attitudes toward property changed as families scattered across a vast country. Instead of keeping property in the family for future generations, it was more likely to be broken up and sold. Democratic ideals influenced inheritance laws in the new United States so that siblings, including daughters, inherited equally.

Democratic ideals of individual happiness and equality began to be discussed in relation to marriage and women. In practice however, women's status remained inferior to that of men. For example, it was not until 1920 that American women gained the right to vote through passage of the nineteenth amendment to the Constitution. The disparity between real life and the revolutionary, **egalitarian** ideals of the latter part of the

---

status—Position or rank, as in society.

egalitarian—Pertaining to the belief in equal access to political, economic, and social rights for all.

eighteenth century applied to race also. Prior to 1800, between 10 and 20 million people were brought from Africa to America in forced servitude.

English tradition had characterized much of colonial life. After 1800, mass migration to the United States from many European countries resulted in American families representing a rich array of racial, ethnic, and national backgrounds. Approximately 19 million people came during the nineteenth century, mainly from northwestern Europe. Between 1890 and 1930, an additional 22 million immigrants arrived from southern and eastern Europe. Native Americans, African Americans, and immigrants from Asia, Mexico, and other parts of the world have added to the diversity of American families.

Industrialization began to take hold in the United States in the early 1800s. Cities developed around factories. The changes from a largely agricultural to an industrial economy and from a rural way of life to an urban one had significant impact on the American family. The workplace became separated from the home. Father, mother, and children no longer worked together. In general, the father assumed responsibility for his family's economic well-being, while the mother was responsible for the management of the home. Young adults could become financially independent of their families by working in factories. It became easier for people to live apart from their families because cities offered them the means to take care of themselves with places to live, eat, shop, and have recreational activities. Women no longer had to depend on a father or a husband to provide a home for them. Some of the family's functions were transferred to hospitals, schools, orphanages, and other agencies that were established to meet the needs of a changing society. As child labor laws were enacted, children, previously valued as farm or factory workers, became more of an economic burden than an asset. City housing was crowded. Schooling for children extended their years of dependence. Smaller families became desirable.

---

industrialization—Process of organizing a society and economy based on large industries and machine production.

Changes in marriage and the family have continued. Ideals of equality embraced by the United States at its founding became the driving force behind the women's **suffrage** movement to secure the vote and the modern women's movement. Women have made significant political, legal, and educational gains during the twentieth century. The trend toward more democratic relationships between men and women has continued. Childrearing has become less **authoritarian**, with greater emphasis placed on the rights of the individual child.

Historical events and social forces exert their influence on family life now as in the past. The changes they bring result in both benefits and costs to each generation. When some family members gain greater control over their lives, other members lose some authority. We now turn to a consideration of the family in contemporary society.

American Families Today

One of the major trends over the past two or three decades is the presence of women with children in the paid workforce, as noted in Chapter One. The decade of the 1990s is the first in which the majority of mothers of young children (more than 50 percent) work outside the home.

U.S. Census Bureau statistics show other trends with implications for those who work with young children and their families. Increasing numbers of parents are having only one or two children. The only child is becoming more common, which means that fewer children than in the past will experience a sibling relationship. Among the reasons for declining family size are delayed marriage and childbearing, the economic demands of raising children, and the need for families to have two incomes to maintain a standard of living that used to be possible with one salary. If marriage and parenthood are postponed for education

---

suffrage—The right to vote in political elections.

authoritarian—Parenting style characterized by the use of control and the expectation of unquestioning obedience.

Figure 4.1 Balancing the demands of work and home is a challenge for many of today's families.

and the establishment of careers, parents are likely to be older and more affluent when their first and perhaps only child is born.

About 50 percent of American marriages end in divorce and of these, three of five involve children. Close to 25 percent of children live in families maintained by one parent. As the result of single parents remarrying, there are approximately seven million children under 18 years of age who are stepchildren.

It is clear that child care, balancing the demands of work and home, single parenting, and adapting to changing family structures are among the issues facing today's families.

The 1990 census also shows changes in immigration patterns. The past decade has seen the number of Asian and Hispanic immigrants double. These families contribute to the richness of

America's diversity, but they find themselves raising children in a **culture** that is unfamiliar to them.

The challenge for the nanny is to understand families in their various forms and situations and the nanny's role in the family support system. The remaining sections of this chapter examine aspects of family life that are important for meeting this challenge successfully.

THE INFLUENCE OF CULTURE, RELIGION, AND SOCIAL CLASS ON FAMILY LIFE

Among the influences on family life, culture, religion, and **social class** play significant roles in determining the **values**, traditions, and childrearing practices of any given family. Woven into the patterns of everyday life, they contribute to the unique character of a family. All of us become accustomed to the family life in which we grow up. The implication for nannies is that family life in the home of their employers will not be exactly the same as it was in the homes in which they grew up. This does not necessarily mean that conflicts will arise, but it does require that nannies be prepared to deal with differences in constructive ways. Approached with respect and sensitivity, differences provide new experiences that make life interesting.

On a personal level, the new environment requires some adjustments on the nanny's part so that confusion about how to act or homesickness do not interfere with settling into the new job and housing arrangements. On a professional level, differences should be accepted as opportunities to learn about and appreciate diversity. By respecting families as unique groups of people, nannies are able to develop better understanding of employing

---

culture—A way of life of a particular group of people encompassing all aspects of life and passed from one generation to another.

social class—Group of people ranked together in society according to economic, educational, and occupational criteria.

values—A social principle or standard held or accepted by an individual, class, or society.

families and forge more effective partnerships with parents to provide consistent care. Nannies also provide a positive role model for children when they show interest in and respect for differing **customs, beliefs,** and ideas.

Culture

Culture is the way of life of a particular group of people. It encompasses all aspects of group life such as skills, arts, customs, and ideas that are passed on from one generation to another. We absorb the culture in which we are raised without being aware of it. Awareness occurs when we come in contact with a culture that differs from our own. Within the family, culture influences many aspects of life such as holiday celebrations, food preferences, manners, how family members show affection to one another, **sex roles,** intergenerational relationships, and customs surrounding births, deaths, and marriages.

A nanny can support children's ethnic heritage and the cultural norms and traditions that arise from it when planning care in such areas as play activities, toy and book selections, meal planning, fostering social skills, and the observance of holidays and other special family events. The employing family may welcome opportunities to learn about other customs from the nanny. Families and nannies can both be enriched by each other's cultural experiences.

Disagreements between nannies and parents sometimes arise because of culturally different childrearing practices. For example, parents may have cultural preferences about how their children should be fed that are very different from practices in mainstream America. Or, parents may be culturally influenced to regard physical punishment as a necessary part of raising children properly. When conflicts arise, it is important for nannies to take the cultural perspective of parents into consideration and to

---

custom—*A social practice passed on by tradition.*

belief—*Acceptance that certain things are true.*

sex role—*Societal or cultural characteristics (masculine or feminine) of one's gender.*

Figure 4.2   Each family and child is unique.

be aware of their own **biases** arising from cultural experience. A question for the nanny to consider would be "Is this practice potentially harmful to the child so that I could not possibly change or compromise on this issue, or am I assuming that my way is the right way when, in fact, a good outcome for the child can be achieved in a variety of ways?" Applying this question to the conflict over how children should be fed, the culturally sensitive nanny concludes that there is no reason not to comply with the parent's preferences, because they are nutritionally sound and children the world over thrive on feeding patterns that differ from prevailing patterns in the United States. With regard to the conflict about physical punishment, the nanny recognizes the cultural perspective from which the parents are coming, but remains firm that the practice is inconsistent with good child care. Since parents have ultimate authority about how to raise their children, the

---

bias—*Prejudice or inclination toward a particular point of view.*

nanny should be alert to serious obstacles to a harmonious relationship while interviewing for a position (see Chapter Eight for interviewing and pages 171–174 for issues to discuss).

The nanny should also be prepared for cultural differences between one region of the United States and another and between one type of community and another. Differences can be expected when a job involves moving from the Midwest to the east or west coast, or from the South to the North, for example. A metropolitan area will be different from a rural community. The pace of life, relationships with neighbors and friends, styles of dress, and food preferences are among the differences likely to be noticed when relocating. An open mind and a spirit of adventure are keys to adjusting successfully and enjoying new experiences.

Religion

The United States is a religiously diverse country where the right to worship or not to worship, as one pleases, is prized. Diversity not only characterizes the variety of religious faiths, but also the importance religious practice plays in the lives of individuals and families. Sometimes overlapping **ethnic** culture, religion influences the family value system, the holidays that are celebrated, **rituals** and traditions, interactions between children and parents, and marriage, and kinship relationships.

Given the religious diversity in the United States, it is quite likely that the nanny's religion will differ from that of the employing family. By identifying similarities and respecting differences, the nanny can work effectively with a family of a different faith.

Religions vary in the extent to which their rituals impact on everyday life. For example, some religions have dietary rules. Certain foods may be prohibited. Food may have to be prepared in a certain way. The nanny who is unfamiliar with these rules learns how to comply with them when planning and preparing

---

ethnic—Pertaining to a group of people distinguished by a common history, customs, language, and other shared characteristics.

ritual—A traditional procedure or ceremony.

children's meals. Holidays, or holy days, vary from one religion to another. It may be appropriate to include customs associated with a holiday in children's activities. There may be special songs, games, foods, stories, decorations for the home, or other customs.

Although religions may differ in the code of behavior followers are expected to observe, there are fundamental moral rules about which most people agree. It is not appropriate for nannies to try to impose their religious beliefs or practices on children or parents. However, nannies do have a role in supporting parents in the task of nurturing children's moral understanding and encouraging behavior that is commonly held to be good and right. Parents usually want their children to be kind, fair, and honest. They want their children to understand that it is wrong to hurt others, violate the rights of others, or take or abuse the property of others. Nannies and parents can work together in fostering moral development by establishing clear expectations for children's behavior, providing age-appropriate guidance and modeling desirable behavior.

A nanny whose own religion carries obligations such as attending services at certain times should keep this in mind when applying for a nanny position. A conflict between the hours parents need child care and the time the nanny needs to be off-duty for religious observances should be avoided. Employers should inform candidates for a nanny position of any religious rituals observed in their home that have relevance to the job. Nannies and employers can support each other's religious practices when there is mutual respect and an understanding of what is involved.

Social Class

Social class refers to the ranking of groups of people in a society according to criteria such as occupation, income, and education. Many facets of family life are influenced by social class, including family values, the socialization of children, **lifestyle**,

---

lifestyle—A person's way of life exemplified by his or her possessions, activities, attitudes, and manner.

the friends and marriage partner one chooses, and relationships with the extended family.

The majority of Americans identify with the middle class, characterized by a comfortable standard of living and, in general, democratic ideals in family relationships. There is, however, considerable variation in lifestyle among middle-class families. The combined incomes of two professionals or success in such fields as computer technology, entertainment, or sports allows some middle-class families an affluent lifestyle far beyond the reach of others. Many of today's nanny employers are two-career couples. Their lifestyles may not be the same as those experienced in the nannies' own families. The employers' home and its furnishings, spending habits, and choices in leisure-time activities, magazines and newspapers, television shows, books, and music may be different. The nanny with a professional approach to the job refrains from comments and criticisms and recognizes opportunities for personal growth in new situations. Basic family values shared by the nanny and employer should be emphasized to strengthen their relationship and minimize differences.

Upper-class families, a term usually applied to those whose wealth and prestige have been well established for several generations, represent a very small proportion of the American population. The nanny who is employed by an upper-class family may be surprised at a tendency toward restraint in the way the family spends money on material possessions. Ostentation is regarded with disfavor. The upper-class family preserves homes, furniture, heirlooms, and other possessions from one generation to another. Interactions between family members are likely to be more formal than in middle-class families. The nanny may be a member of a large household staff, with the nanny–employer relationship also more formal. To the extent that this type of lifestyle is unfamiliar to the nanny, adjustments and a willingness to learn from new experiences will be necessary.

Books that explore diversity, including activity books for children, are suggested in Appendix E.

PARENTING STYLES AND SITUATIONS

Parenting is the parent's work of raising a child. It encompasses many aspects of the childrearing process and includes providing children with affection, nurturance, and **discipline**. For nannies to be able to support parents in this work, an understanding of various parenting approaches and situations is necessary. Parents and nannies need to be in reasonable agreement about childrearing practices in order to work together and provide consistency for children. Nannies need to understand the adjustments that first-time parents have to make and the challenges faced by dual-career parents, single parents, stepparents, and adoptive parents. Nannies must also be aware of the role of grandparents in the family.

Parenting Styles

Parents tend to raise their children as they themselves were raised. Often unconsciously, they model their parenting behavior on the behavior of their own parents. This is not to imply that childrearing approaches do not change. Parents are influenced not only by their own experiences as children, but by changes in society's attitude toward children, the advice of contemporary authorities in the field of child health and development, and their own particular family needs. In each generation, parents develop their own parenting styles derived from a variety of influences.

A study of parenting styles and their effects on children's socialization by Diana Baumrind (1978) provides a helpful way to look at various childrearing approaches. She described parenting styles as being authoritarian, **permissive**, or **authoritative**. The

---

discipline—Guidance that leads a child toward socially acceptable behavior and self-control.

permissive—Parenting style characterized by little parental guidance or direction.

authoritative—Parenting style characterized by firm but reasonable limits, prudent guidance, and respect for the child's individuality.

authoritarian style is characterized by close regulation of the child's behavior. Unquestioning compliance with rules is expected. The restrictions imposed on the child give little opportunity for practicing decision-making skills. The permissive style, on the other hand, allows the child to make most of the decisions and provides few guidelines for behavior. Children of permissive parents tend to be immature and lacking in self-control.

The authoritative style lies between the extremes of the authoritarian and permissive styles of parenting. Authoritative parents balance the need to provide children with firm, consistent discipline with the need to encourage children to become independent and responsible for their own behavior. Authoritative parents respect the child's **autonomy**, but do not abdicate their obligation to set reasonable limits. However, these parents are willing to consider a child's request to alter rules on occasion. Parental rights and children's rights are both recognized. As a result, children of authoritative parents are likely to develop competence, self-reliance, and self-control.

Most parents do not fall neatly into one of these categories of parenting styles. Their style may be anywhere along a continuum from authoritarian to permissive. Striking a balance between too much and too little intervention presents a challenge for parents, nannies, and everyone involved in the care and nurture of young children.

First-Time Parents

The arrival of the first baby brings new responsibilities, tasks, roles, and priorities to parents. It marks the beginning of the childrearing stage of family life when individual and marital interests have to be reorganized to meet the demands of raising a child. Adjustments in the way time, energy, and money are spent are necessary. When and whether the mother should return to paid employment and making satisfactory child-care arrangements are important issues for many of today's new parents. Decisions

---

autonomy—Sense of independence and the ability to make one's own decisions.

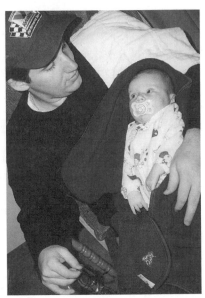

Figure 4.3 New responsibilities, tasks, roles and priorities come with first-time parenthood.

about how the care of the baby and the house will be shared also must be made, since these are no longer widely regarded as a woman's responsibility alone.

There are special challenges and rewards for the nanny who works with a family shortly after the arrival of the first baby. The nanny's skills in newborn care and sensitivity to the needs of new parents can ease the transition into parenthood. When helping parents with the baby, the nanny must be careful not to come between the parents and the baby, regardless of the parents' inexperience. Parents need to gain confidence in their ability to perceive their baby's needs and care for her. Their task is to form an **attachment** with their baby. This involves getting to know her and responding to her. The nanny helps this process by providing support and by knowing when not to intervene. Guidance about baby care should be offered tactfully and good techniques modeled.

---

attachment—*An affectionate bond that develops between a child and another person that joins them emotionally.*

The nanny can also help ensure an environment in which the mother can adjust to her role as a mother while recuperating from the childbirth experience. Rest, sleep, and nutrition are important during the **postpartum** period. The nanny's hours may need to be altered temporarily to prevent the mother from becoming exhausted from night feedings. The mother should be encouraged to take care of herself and follow the instructions of her obstetrician.

Sometime during the postpartum period, the mother may experience a let-down feeling commonly called the "**baby blues**." Usually very temporary, this condition produces irritability and tears for no apparent reason and is thought to be the result of the hormonal and emotional upheavals that occur after delivery. Discomfort and fatigue may be contributing factors. Allowing the tears to flow usually relieves tension and brings comfort. If the mother is embarrassed by her unexplained emotional display, the nanny needs to be kind and understanding. The mother can be reassured that crying is perfectly acceptable and will probably make her feel better. If the blues persist, a physician should be consulted.

Parental leave following the birth of the baby may be as short as six weeks or extend to three or four months. The new mother who anticipated returning to work after six weeks may very well find herself wanting additional time with her baby after the birth. Sometimes the father is the parent who takes leave to care for the new baby. More often it is the mother who is faced with the conflict between wanting to be with her baby and wanting to maintain a career.

The nanny needs to be sensitive to the adjustments parents have to make when they entrust their child to someone else's care for large portions of the day. Ideally, there is overlap between the time the nanny begins to work and the time the mother

---

postpartum—Occurring after childbirth.

baby blues—Colloquial term used to describe the temporary let-down, miserable feeling commonly experienced by mothers about four days after childbirth.

returns to work. The mother can gradually become accustomed to leaving the baby in the nanny's care for increasing lengths of time before having to be away at work all day. Coordinating breastfeeding with the mother's absences can be practiced, so that it may be more easily continued by the working mother. Good communications between the nanny and the parents help parents to feel involved in their child's life even when they are away and confident in the care the nanny provides (communications are discussed in Chapter Five). The transition to work is eased when the nanny demonstrates a commitment to supporting the new family as well as caring for the baby.

Dual-Career Parents

Being dual-career parents presents both rewards and challenges. On the positive side, the marriage relationship may be enhanced when both partners have the feeling of accomplishment that comes from a career. Another benefit to the relationship may be the sharing of ideas, experiences, and social and business relationships gained from the workplace. Mothers, traditionally the parent who stayed at home with the children, may feel they can do a better job of parenting because of the stimulation of work outside the home and the sense of fulfillment a career brings. Two incomes can help alleviate anxiety about the cost of raising children in these times of economic uncertainty. Lessons in self-reliance, responsibility, and equality of the sexes may be easier to instill in children when mother and father both have careers and everyone has a share in making home life run smoothly.

On the negative side, a feeling of never having enough time or energy to do everything that has to be done is common among working parents. Like other skills, though, balancing the demands of family and work takes practice, but it can be learned. Today's busy families have to have realistic expectations about what they can accomplish, set priorities, remain flexible, and develop a network of support. Leaving their children is often the most difficult part of working outside the home for mothers, particularly when children are very young. The prospect of missing developmental milestones and other events in the child's life is hard to contemplate. Concerns about the effect of the mother's absence on the child's emotional development or the child's safety in someone else's care are typical. Mothers may experience considerable ambivalence and guilt about giving up full-time care of their young children for a career.

Finding reliable, quality child care is clearly a major factor in resolving some of the difficulty of leaving children while away at work. Both fathers and mothers adjust more easily to the demands of dual-career parenting when they have child-care arrangements they can trust. However, alternative arrangements must be in readiness in the event the nanny is ill or unavailable for some other reason, or if the child who attends a day care program is ill. Alternate caregivers or willing neighbors or relatives need to be identified before this situation occurs, since most employers do not provide parental leave for child-care emergencies.

When both parents have demanding jobs, reserving time to nurture themselves and their own relationship is important for family well-being. In some nanny employment arrangements, provision is made for the nanny to care for the children for an occasional weekend, so parents can have time for themselves away from home.

Although a nanny is not responsible for running the entire household, contributing to a smooth-running home is part of a nanny's job. Parents will appreciate returning from work to a home that is orderly, where toys have been picked up, dishes washed, and clothing put away in the correct place. Children should be reasonably clean for their parents' arrival and diapers should be changed. Time should be allowed for the transfer of child-care responsibilities from the nanny to the parents when they come home from work each day. This makes the transition easier for the children as well as for parents and everyone benefits. In addition, telephone messages taken by the nanny should be passed on promptly and accurately. Breakages, items in need of repair, and groceries or other supplies that need replenishing should be noted and reported in a timely way.

Trying to help a young child understand what parents do at work can be difficult. Some jobs—such as physician, nurse, or flight attendant—lend themselves to pretend play for the older toddler or preschooler. Work that involves being in an office much of the time is more difficult to explain to a young child. A parent who works in an advertising agency, for example, might relate her work to commercials that the child sees on television. The nanny can reinforce parents' explanations with books and games and by talking with the child about what mommy and daddy are doing at work at any given time. It may help to display a photograph of the parent in his or her work setting where the child can easily see it. Sometimes parents can arrange for their children to visit the workplace.

Single-Parent Families

A single-parent family may be the result of the death of a parent, divorce, or the parent never having been married. Liberalized adoption laws make it easier for a single person to adopt a child. Whatever the circumstances, single parents face responsibilities that include being both mother and father to the children, running the household, and providing for the family.

Social isolation and loneliness are not unusual among single parents, particularly during the first few months after a divorce or death. Friends, especially married couples, may not include a single person in their social activities. Loyalties among friends may be strained in the case of a divorce. New responsibilities and roles, as well as adjusting to the loss of a marriage partner, can also interfere with a social life. Programs such as Parents Without Partners (see Appendix F) have been organized to help address social isolation, loneliness, and other issues of concern to single parents.

Those who work with young children must be sensitive to the particular needs of single-parent families. For example, early childhood programs and schools can help single parents' involvement in their children's education by scheduling parent/teacher conferences and other events at times when single parents are available. Important for all working parents, reliable child care is critical for the parent raising children alone. Good child care also helps provide stability for children whose lives have been disrupted by divorce or a parent's death. A nanny can be a valuable source of support in a single-parent family, but must take care to maintain a professional role and avoid inappropriate friendship with the parent. A nonjudgmental attitude toward single-parent families is also necessary for professional effectiveness in this situation.

Stepparenting

Stepparenting occurs in a family in which there is an adult couple with at least one of the adults having a child from a previous marriage. Such families are called stepfamilies. "Blended" is another term used to describe stepfamilies, but it may be misleading. Since stepfamilies result from loss and bring children and adults with different pasts under one roof, it is probably unrealistic to expect them to become truly "blended."

The role of the stepparent is not always clear. A stepparent cannot replace the child's own parent, but can become an important person in the child's life. Patience and flexibility are necessary for building the new relationship successfully. A stepparent can enrich children's lives by sharing activities with them that do not compete with the absent parent. Spousal support is essential. Parents in stepfamilies need to back each other up on matters of discipline and household rules. Family traditions, important to a child's sense of security, need to be incorporated into new family patterns so birthdays, holidays, and other occasions are celebrated in familiar ways. Given time, new family traditions may emerge as the stepfamily develops its own way of doing things.

The **extended family** is likely to grow when a stepfamily forms. Step relatives that include grandparents, cousins, aunts, and uncles may be acquired. The family network can become quite large and complicated, particularly when more than one stepfamily is involved. Children may have to deal with new sibling positions in the stepfamily. Other adjustments may include moving to a new home and school.

The nanny who works for a stepfamily can support parents' efforts to create a home favorable to strengthening new relation-

---

extended family—Family unit consisting of parents, children, grandparents, and other relatives, such as aunts and uncles.

ships. The child's loyalty to the absent parent must be respected. Stepfamilies have their own unique composition. They are not all at the same stage of evolving into comfortable, caring relationships. The Stepfamily Association of America, with chapters in major cities, offers information and support (see Appendix F). Books about stepfamilies are listed in Appendix E.

Adoptive Parenting

Adoption offers a way to become a parent when it is not possible through birth or marriage. Adoptions are usually arranged through public or private agencies, or independently through the services of an attorney. Some agencies specialize in international or interracial adoptions. Adoptive parents have often wanted to be parents for a long time and have experienced the disappointment of discovering they are unlikely to be biological parents. Once the decision to adopt has been made, the wait for an available child may be long.

Adoptive parents often have more concerns about the child's genetic history, prenatal health, and personality than if the child was biologically theirs. They may have additional concerns if the child is from another country or racial background. In common with all new parents, adoptive parents have to accept the particular child for the individual he or she is. Sound and sympathetic medical advice can help allay unnecessary fears about the child's health and guide parents' understanding of the child's behavior and temperament.

When working with adoptive parents, the nanny should find out how they want their child's questions about adoption handled. Typically, the young child is curious about his birth mother and why she gave him away. The school-age child may blame herself for being given up and may fear that her stay with her adoptive family will not be permanent. Parents are usually advised to maintain honest and ongoing discussion with the child and provide information and reassurance according to the child's level of understanding. Each family situation is unique and the nanny needs to become aware of the particular parents' approach and the nanny's role in supporting it.

Adolescents may become increasingly interested in their birth parents and want to find out who they are. By recognizing that such interests are consistent with an adolescent's normal search for identity, adoptive parents are not so likely to feel hurt or rejected when this happens. The actual search for more information about birth parents is usually delayed until children become adults.

Adoption is not a one-time legal event, but a lifelong process for everyone involved. Contact with other adoptive families and getting to know others in the same situation can help an adoptive child feel less different. Support groups also provide parents with opportunities to share experiences and learn from one another.

Adoptive Families of America (see Appendix F) offers helpful information on many aspects of adoption. Books about adoption for adults and children are listed in Appendix E.

Grandparents

Grandparents can occupy a very special place in the lives of children. Free of the immediate responsibilities of childrearing, they can help their own children and their grandchildren in ways that enrich family life and preserve family togetherness. Grandparents offer children new experiences, pass on family traditions and values, and are often the organizers of family reunions and holiday celebrations.

Adult children sometimes feel ambivalent about their parents' involvement as grandparents. Struggling to develop a sense of competence, first-time parents may feel threatened by a grandparent's skill with a young child. There may be a concern that the child prefers the company of indulgent grandparents to that of his parents. Differences of opinion about how things should be done may arise. Grandparents should avoid telling their own children what to do. Any discussion about childrearing matters must be done tactfully and out of the child's hearing. Rather than offering advice or criticism, grandparents can be most effective by modeling desirable behavior for both parent and child.

The nanny's relationship with grandparents should be pleasant but professional. When grandparents come to stay for a visit, the parents and the nanny need to discuss in advance how the nanny's routines with the children may be affected, together with anything else relevant to ensuring a happy time for everyone. If a comfortable relationship exists between grandparents and their adult children, the grandparents' relationship with the nanny is likely to be a positive one. If disagreements do arise concerning the care of the child, the nanny must remember that parents have ultimate authority for deciding what is best for their children and tactfully defer to the parents' wishes. The nanny must guard against talking inappropriately with the grandparents about the parents, the nanny's employers.

See Appendix E for suggested further reading on various parenting situations. Information about the Family and Medical Leave Act of 1993 may be of interest to working parents coping with childrearing and other family responsibilities and may be obtained by calling 1–800–959–3652.

DIVORCE

About half of all marriages in the United States end in divorce. Although so common, it is a painful process for a family to go through, particularly when children are involved. Regardless of how much conflict existed between their parents during the marriage, children usually fear and resent divorce. The most important factors in a child's ability to cope successfully are the continued affection, interest, and support of both parents.

Grief, anger, guilt, and disbelief are typical reactions to the losses and changes associated with divorce. Children often do not express these feelings in ways that adults understand or approve. Nevertheless, adults need to listen to children in emotionally painful situations and offer reassurance and information appropriate to the child's level of understanding. Children want to know what is going to happen to them and that they still have two loving parents. Open, honest communication and patience with sometimes difficult behavior help children deal with the distress of divorce and eventually regain a sense of well-being.

---

grief—*Intense emotional pain and sadness resulting from a significant loss or other extremely distressing event.*

Young children find it hard to grasp the concept of divorce and may believe that they are to blame for a parent's departure from home. They may be afraid that the other parent will leave too, giving rise to tears and tantrums at bedtime or other temporary separations. **Regressive behavior** may be observed. Older children may also blame themselves for the divorce. They often cling to the hope that their parents will reconcile and refuse to believe the divorce is anything but a temporary rift. They may speak to others about their family as if their mother and father were still together. School performance may decline. Unusual rebelliousness, hostile or destructive behavior, lack of interest in friends and play, or changes in sleeping and eating patterns may also indicate children's unhappiness and stress. If signs of stress persist, professional counseling may be necessary.

The first year of a divorce is usually the hardest. For most children, the fear, confusion, anger and grief gradually diminish. Adults overcome the immediate devastation of the divorce and learn to mobilize strengths for moving on with their lives. The relationship with the custodial parent is extremely important for the child's adjustment to the new situation. The child needs dependable parental care, love, and guidance for security. The child also needs the continued involvement of the noncustodial parent, unhindered by any negative feelings the two parents may have for one another. The child's sense of security can also be strengthened by ongoing contact with grandparents and other relatives, remaining in the same residence if possible, keeping the same child-care arrangements, attending the same school and place of worship, and maintaining the same friendships.

Divorce involves legal as well as emotional issues. Principal among these are money arrangements and child **custody** decisions.

---

regressive behavior—*Renewal of behavior from which a child had developmentally advanced, such as toileting accidents, thumb sucking, or wanting a bottle.*

custody—*Legal responsibility for the care, protection, and nurture of a child.*

Child support payments are determined by the court so that the noncustodial parent contributes to the child's financial support. Child custody involves deciding who will have legal responsibility for decisions affecting the child and for providing everyday care and nurture. Custody law varies from state to state. There are several types of arrangements.

In *single-parent custody*, one parent has full responsibility for the child, even when the child spends time with the noncustodial parent. The parent with custody may be either the mother or the father, depending on who requests custody and what the court determines is in the best interests of the child.

Joint custody divides the responsibility between the parents, with the child living alternately with one parent for a certain period of time and then with the other parent.

In a *split custody* arrangement the children are split between the parents, each parent having single-parent custody of some of the children.

Third-party custody occurs when neither parent is capable of or wants to care for the child. The court awards custody to a relative, appoints a guardian, or places the child through a public agency.

A nanny who comes in contact with divorce in the course of employment must be sensitive to the emotional needs of children who have experienced or are experiencing this crisis in their lives. The nanny must also be aware of custody arrangements, including provisions for children to visit with the noncustodial parent. When a nanny works for a stepfamily, it is possible that a parent (or both parents) is the noncustodial parent of children from a previous marriage. In that event, the nanny must be prepared for children's visits to their noncustodial parent. These visits may be short or may be for vacations and holidays. The nanny's responsibilities for the care of the visiting children should be defined in advance.

Books about divorce for adults and children are listed in Appendix E.

DEATH IN THE FAMILY

Of all the losses and separations experienced by children and adults, death is the most difficult. Death is final, the loss is permanent. It is very hard for children to understand. Many adults are afraid of death and uncomfortable in its presence. In order to help children cope with death, adults have to come to terms with their own fears and discomfort about it.

The reaction to a painful event such as death or other significant loss often includes shock and disbelief, anger, guilt, and overwhelming sadness. Physical distress is common—the hollow feeling inside, the lump in the throat, fatigue, loss of appetite, and insomnia. Grief can be felt for a long time, but normally these feelings are worked through, the loss accepted, and the strength found to move on with life.

Children feel the loss and bewilderment that adults do when faced with a death, but they understand it and show their grief differently. Children can get overlooked in the shock and confusion that surround a death in the family. They need reassurance that they will be taken care of and have their questions answered. Children cannot be sheltered from life's painful experiences, but a supportive adult's willingness to try to explain what is happening is reassuring in itself. If questions are evaded or signs of distress ignored, the child gets the message that the topic is too dreadful to discuss or that it is unacceptable to show feelings.

The child's age, who the lost person was, and whether the death was sudden or the result of a long illness influence how a child perceives the death. As time passes and as the child grows older, perceptions will change. The need to explore the topic further and ask questions will continue.

Young children view death as temporary and reversible. They may ask over and over again when grandpa is coming back. They need simple, straightforward information to help them understand that the person died, he will not come back, and we are sad because we miss him. If questions arise about burial or cremation, the child needs to know that the dead person cannot feel or be hurt, cannot speak, and is no longer as we knew him. Older children may persist in believing that the person is still alive and display little or no sign of grief. If denial and avoidance of grief are prolonged, emotional problems may become evident later.

Feelings of guilt are not uncommon when someone close dies. Adults regret that they did not give more time or affection to the person, make up after a quarrel, or see how serious an illness was. Children may also experience guilt. Unable to distinguish between real and pretend, young children believe they have the power to cause events that happen around them, even by just wishing something to happen. Having once wished a sibling or a parent dead, the child feels responsible and guilty when the wish becomes a reality. Children may believe their own behavior caused parents to divorce or a grandparent to become ill. They need reassurance that they are not to blame.

Anger is a natural reaction to the feelings of abandonment and insecurity that result from losing someone close. Anger may be directed at the dead person or surviving relatives. Children may show anger in disruptive behavior at home or in school. Tantrums and irritability may be more frequent.

Children sometimes act out their struggle to cope with death in pretend play and should be allowed to do so. Regressive behavior, nightmares, and fear of being alone may occur. Feelings of sadness are likely to surface on and off for a long period of time.

Sometimes professional counseling is necessary to help a child through the grieving process. Indications that this might be advisable include prolonged loss of interest in daily activities and friends, insomnia and loss of appetite, significant decline in school performance, or refusal to go to school. If a child witnesses a violent death, professional help is recommended.

It is not unusual for nannies to encounter a death in the course of their work with families. The nanny can help children feel safe and well cared for in the face of death and the confusion that surrounds it. For bereaved adults, the nanny can be a source of emotional support and practical help. The way that a family deals with death in accordance with its culture, religious beliefs, and preferences must be respected.

In expressing sympathy to a bereaved family, a simple "I am so sorry" and a warm touch or hug are more helpful than trying to rationalize or improve the situation. It does not comfort a person dealing with loss to be told "It was for the best" when someone has died from a serious illness, or "You have your other children" when a child has died or a baby is stillborn. Regardless of the circumstances, death brings shock and sadness, and it is by responding to these feelings that sympathy is best offered. Listening to the survivor speak of the dead person and the circumstances of the death, often over and over again, can be helpful. The repeated storytelling enables the survivor to grasp the reality of the death. There are many moods and expressions of grief for adults as there are for children.

Those who work with children and families must be prepared to deal with death and confront their own feelings about it. Children are curious about death even when they have not experienced a devastating personal loss. Questions may be provoked by the dead bird discovered in the garden. The death of a family pet creates opportunities to talk about sad feelings and what happens when death occurs. Books about death for adults and children are suggested in Appendix E.

THE NANNY/CHILD/PARENT RELATIONSHIPS

This chapter has explored many aspects of family life to which nannies can be exposed during their work in private homes. In this section, relationships between the nanny and the child and the parent are considered. Every professional who provides a service to others must develop a relationship with clients. In child care, effective relationships must be developed with both the child and the parent(s).

The Nanny/Child Relationship

At the center of the relationship between the nanny and the child is the attachment that young children need to establish with their caregivers. Attachment develops through caregiving interactions. It involves being close to a child and responsive to her

Figure 4.4 Special times together make a child feel cared about as well as taken care of.
(Courtesy Murray State College, Tishomingo, Oklahoma)

needs. It makes a child feel she is cared about as well as taken care of. However, the nanny must not infringe on the parent/child relationship and always remembers that parents are the primary caregivers and teachers of their children. The following guidelines suggest ways in which the nanny can develop a close, responsive relationship with the child while supporting the parent/child relationship.

Build a trust relationship. When children's physical and psychological needs are met in respectful, responsive ways, they develop trust in the caregiver and the security they need to explore, discover, and learn. Babies usually form a primary attachment with their mothers. Because of the trend toward greater involvement of fathers with their babies, there is often a strong attachment to fathers, too. When young children are cared for by adults other than their parents for substantial parts of the day, secondary attachments with these caregivers become very important for the child's emotional development also.

Remember that the nanny's relationship is temporary. Important though the nanny's role may be in a young child's life, the child's attachment to caregivers is not the same as attachment to parents. The most obvious difference is that attachment to parents is long-term. Beginning at birth, parents are a permanent force in their children's lives. From the start of any job, a nanny has to accept that caring for this particular child will come to an end one day. The relationship will change even though nannies often maintain contact with families for whom they worked in the past. The anticipated duration of the relationship makes a significant difference between being a nanny and being a parent.

Contribute to the parent/child relationship. Let parents know the personality traits, talents, and other strengths that you find appealing in the child. It pleases parents to know that others enjoy their child. It helps to enhance their perception of the child and contributes to positive feelings about being a parent. Support the child's natural pride in his parents, too. A nanny must never say or do anything that would diminish parents in their child's eyes. Help parents and children to enjoy one another when they are reunited at the end of the parents' work day. Plan for a smooth transition, allowing parents time to adjust before they take over child-care responsibilities from you.

The Nanny/Parent Relationship

Everyone benefits when the nanny and the parents develop an effective working relationship. Children thrive where there is continuity of care from the adults who are important in their lives. Parents' trust in the nanny grows when the parent/nanny team is working well. For the nanny, a harmonious relationship is essential for promoting children's well-being to the fullest extent possible and for job satisfaction. The following guidelines suggest ways in which the nanny can foster positive relationships with parents.

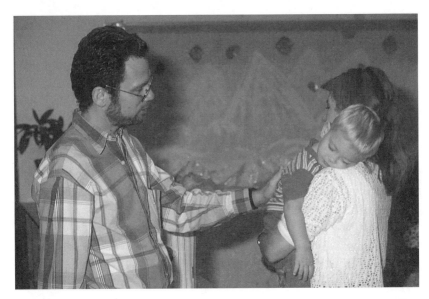

Figure 4.5 Everyone benefits from an effective working relationship between the nanny and parents.

Understand your role in the household. Begin by being clear in your own mind about why you have chosen to care for someone else's children in someone else's home. The role of the nanny and the parent must not be confused. The nanny is there to complement the parent, not to replace. Mothers in particular often feel ambivalent or guilty about going out to work and leaving their children in someone else's care. They worry that their children will become closer to the caregiver than to them. Suspicions that this is happening, unfounded or not, will undermine the relationship between the nanny and the mother. Nannies must never compete, or seem to be competing with parents for children's affections. The parent/child relationship must be supported. Nannies must also be able to make a clear distinction between the relationships they form in their employer's family and their relationships within their own families. Nannies must be able to share in the many aspects of family life likely to be encountered in a private home without compromising their professionalism. Though nannies may feel for the joys and sorrows of the families who employ them, they must maintain some detachment to be effective. Personal friendships with either parent, other family members, or friends of the family complicate the nanny/parent relationship, confuse children, and are inappropriate.

Respect parents. Raising children requires many years of commitment, sacrifice, and responsibility. Parents deserve respect for the job of parenting. Theirs is the primary role in promoting their children's healthy development. They are their children's primary caregivers and teachers. It is sometimes tempting for those who take care of other people's children to criticize parents for the way they parent. Whether the criticism is voiced or not, a judgmental attitude toward parents will inhibit the nanny/parent relationship. Nannies must avoid seeing themselves as superior substitutes for parents or the rescuers of children whose parents are too busy to take care of them. Instead, nannies need to see themselves as parent supports in the task of promoting children's well-being. The values, needs, and ideas of parents must be acknowledged when there is disagreement about childrearing issues. Professional expertise must not be used to impose the nanny's ideas on parents, but to work together with parents toward a reasonable solution.

Develop a partnership with parents. A partnership between the nanny and parents provides the child with needed consistency and strengthens the nanny/parent relationship. Conflicts over discipline and decisions concerning the child are avoided when the nanny and parent develop a system of mutual support. Children are confused when they receive contradictory messages from the nanny and a parent. The parent and the nanny need to discuss and agree upon how they will respond in certain situations before the situations arise. While the nanny may be in charge of daily routines and activities, the parent will probably be the one who decides if a child can invite a friend for dinner or spend some of his piggy-bank money. When the nanny and the parent are involved with the children at the same time, it is particularly important that they support one another. For example, a child's request for a cookie is denied by the nanny because it is close to lunchtime. The mother enters the room, the same request is made and she approves. The result is that the nanny's authority is undermined and the child is encouraged to play the mother and the nanny against each other to get what he wants in the future. The nanny and the parent need to check with one another before responding to such requests. The parent and the nanny should uphold one another's decisions in front of the child, even though there may be disagreement. The matter should be discussed later out of the child's hearing.

Exercise tact. Although you may be included in many family activities in your work situation, there will be times when it will be tactful for you to withdraw and leave family members on their own. For example, you see your employers engaged in a quiet husband-and-wife chat or involved in an argument, or parents are interacting with a child. These are not times to interrupt except in a real emergency. The tactful nanny withdraws. Even though you may often be included in family meals or invited to join the family to watch television in the evening, it is better not to become dependent on this. Give the family opportunities to be by themselves as a family from time to time. Nannies cannot expect to be included in all special family events. They need to develop a sense of when they are truly welcome and when it would be better to make other plans. Privacy is important for both nannies and families. The presence of a nanny, especially in a live-in situation, requires some sacrifice of privacy for families. This can place a strain on relationships between family members and on nanny/parent relationships unless the nanny recognizes when not to intrude.

Communicate effectively with parents. Good communications are central to every relationship. There are many ways to promote the nanny/parent relationship through good communications and these are discussed extensively in the next chapter.

BIBLIOGRAPHY

Artlip, M.A., Artlip, J.A., and Saltzman, E.S. (1993). *The New American Family*. Lancaster, PA: Starburst Publishers.

Baumrind, D. (1978). "Parental disciplinary patterns and social competence in children." *Youth and Society*, 9, 239–276.

Brazelton, T.B. (1989). *Families: Crisis and Caring.* Reading, MA: Addison-Wesley Publishing Company.

Brazelton, T.B. (1985). *Working and Caring.* Reading, MA: Addison-Wesley Publishing Company.

Breese, C., and Gomer, H. (1988). *The Good Nanny Guide.* London, UK: Century Hutchinson Ltd.

Elicker, J., and Fortner-Wood, C. (1995). "Adult-Child Relationships in Early Childhood Programs." *Young Children* 51(1), 69–78.

Galinsky, E. (1987). *The Six Stages of Parenthood.* Reading, MA: Addison-Wesley Publishing Company.

Goldman, L. (1996). "We Can Help Children Grieve: A Child-Oriented Model for Memorializing." *Young Children* 51(6), 69–73.

Jones, E., and Derman-Sparks, L. (1992). "Meeting the Challenge of Diversity." *Young Children* 47(2), 12–17.

Klaus, M.K., and Kennell, J.H. (1982). *Parent-Infant Bonding,* second edition. St. Louis, MO: C.V. Mosby Company.

Leslie, G.R., and Korman, S.K. (1989). *The Family in Social Context,* seventh edition. New York: Oxford University Press.

Magagna, J. (1986). "Aspects of the Mother/Nanny Relationship: Some concepts from psychoanalytic research to understand problems which can interfere with the optimal care for children." Paper delivered at the International Nanny Conference, August 1986, Scripps College, Claremont, CA.

Murdock, C.V. (1980). *Single Parents are People, Too!* New York: Butterick Publishing.

Schafer, D., and Lyons, C. (1986). *How Do We Tell the Children?* New York: Newmarket Press.

Skolrick, A.S., and Skolrick, J.H. (1992). *Family in Transition,* seventh edition. New York: Harper Collins Publishers.

Thomas, M. (1991). *Balancing Career and Family: Overcoming the Superwoman Syndrome.* Shawnee Mission, KS: National Seminars Publication.

U.S. Bureau of the Census (1991). *Household and Family Characteristics: March 1989 and 1990.* Washington, DC: U.S. Government Printing Office.

U.S. Bureau of the Census (1991). Marital Status and Living Arrangements, March 1990. *Current Population Reports* Series P-20, No 450. Washington, DC: U.S. Government Printing Office.

U.S. Bureau of the Census (1993). 1990 *Census of Population and Housing—Guide Part B. Glossary.* Washington, DC: U.S. Government Printing Office.

U.S. Department of Human Services (1981). *Caring About Kids: When Parents Divorce.* Rockville, MD: National Institute of Mental Health.

Visher, E., and Visher, J. (1982). *How to Win as a Stepfamily.* New York: Dember Books.

Watkins, M., and Fisher, S. (1993). *Talking with Young Children about Adoption.* New Haven, CT: Yale University Press.

Weisberger, E. (1987). *When Your Child Needs You.* Bethesda, MD: Adler and Adler Publishers.

Witmer, D.S., and Honig, A.S. (1994). "Encouraging Positive Social Development in Young Children." *Young Children* 49(5), 4–12.

Chapter 5

Communications

TOPICS

- Introduction
- The Written Employment Agreement
- Keeping the Daily Log
- Daily Reports and Transitions

- Regular Parent/Nanny Conferences
- Job Performance Review
- Guidelines for Effective Communications

Terms to Know

communication   *personal hygiene*
contract   *body language*

INTRODUCTION

The importance of developing a good working relationship with employers has been emphasized in earlier chapters. Effective, ongoing **communication** between the nanny and the employing family is a fundamental component of this relationship. Specific ways for nannies and employers to communicate are examined in this chapter.

Communication is the means by which information is given or exchanged, ideas and feelings are expressed, problems are discussed, and solutions are explored. There are many ways for nannies and employers to communicate.

THE WRITTEN EMPLOYMENT AGREEMENT

Essential to a good working relationship is a clear understanding of the rights and responsibilities of both the employee and the employer. This understanding should always be articulated in a written employment agreement, sometimes referred to as a **contract**. The written agreement puts the relationship between the nanny and the employing family on a professional foundation where it belongs. It helps both parties to clarify and express what each expects from the employment relationship. Misunderstandings are avoided and problems more easily resolved when there is a written agreement for reference.

---

communication—*Giving or exchanging information in any way, such as speech, gestures, writing.*

contract—*A formal, written agreement between two or more people to do certain things.*

There should be a written employment agreement before work begins and the nanny should have a copy. The agreement should be reviewed from time to time and may be altered at any time by mutual consent.

There are certain basic areas that should be covered in any employment agreement. These areas are described on pages 154 and 155 and you should become familiar with them before interviewing for a nanny position. The details of the written agreement will vary from one nanny position to another. A suggested form that can be adapted to the individual situation appears in Appendix A. The importance of a written employment agreement, including a detailed job description, cannot be overstated. No nanny should begin work without one.

KEEPING THE DAILY LOG

There are several reasons why a daily log contributes to good communications between the nanny and the employer. Parents who are away all day need information about their child's daily experiences, health, and development. The written log enables the nanny to organize this information and ensure that it is transmitted to parents. Parents appreciate knowing about special experiences, too, such as a child's reaction to seeing a rainbow or trying a new food. For continuity of care, parents can refer to the log after the nanny is off duty. Over time, the log provides an interesting record of the child's health and development and can be helpful in the early identification of possible problems.

The log provides documentation of the nanny's care and observations. It demonstrates that the nanny is fulfilling the obligations of the job in the parents' absence. Parents can write specific instructions in the log. The nanny should record that these were carried out. This is particularly important if the child requires medication or other treatment while in the nanny's care. The nanny should always record any accident or concern about the child's health, even though it may seem minor at the time. Parents should be informed about *anything* unusual that happens or is observed during their absence.

The log can also be used to note other matters that employers should know about, such as household items that need repair or replacement, or new safety measures or equipment necessary for the growing child.

Examples of daily log forms, one for use with infants and the other for toddlers and preschoolers, are shown in Appendix B. Forms may be hole-punched and kept in a ring notebook in a safe place convenient to the nanny and the parents. The log should be kept throughout the day, with new information added promptly. A separate log should be used for each child and include information about meals and snacks, elimination, activities and outings, **personal hygiene**, and rest. Describe events and observations factually. For example, instead of stating "ate pretty well," describe what the child ate and what was refused. Writing should be neat, legible, and in pen. Corrections should be made by putting a single line through words to be changed, rather than erasing or using correction fluid.

DAILY REPORTS AND TRANSITIONS

Whenever responsibility for the care of the child transfers from the parent to the nanny, or from the nanny to the parent, there should be a comfortable transition including a brief, verbal exchange of information. Usually this happens twice a day, in the morning when parents leave for work and in the evening when they return home. Like the written log, verbal reports help parents and the nanny to ensure the best possible care for the child.

When providing parents with a short verbal summary of the child's day before going off duty, the nanny has an opportunity to share enthusiasm for the child's accomplishments and demonstrate concern for the child's well-being in a way that does not

---

personal hygiene—*Personal habits contributing to health, such as handwashing, bathing/showering, care of teeth, nails and hair, and wearing clean clothing.*

come across in a written log. Parents want to know that the nanny enjoys taking care of their child. They want to feel that the nanny is also concerned about them by facilitating smooth transitions when they leave and return.

The transition will be eased for returning parents if time is allowed for them to settle back into the home environment before the nanny goes off duty. Telephone message, written when they are taken, should be passed on. Any pressing household matter, such as an appliance in need of repair, should be mentioned in the verbal report even if it is noted in the log.

The parent needs to provide the nanny with pertinent information about the child and household when the nanny takes charge. For example, it is helpful for the nanny to know if the child has not slept as usual or the time of the baby's last feeding. If there have been signs of illness or an injury has occurred since the nanny was on duty, the parent should inform the nanny. The nanny should record any unusual information about the child on the back of the log, indicating by whom the information was given and the date and time it was given. Listen carefully to what a parent tells you about a child. Do not hesitate to ask for more information or written directions when needed to ensure safe, appropriate care.

REGULAR PARENT/NANNY CONFERENCES

Daily reports are usually limited to a quick briefing between the nanny and the parent so that both are kept current on day-to-day information affecting the child's well-being and the smooth running of the home. Constraints of time and energy at the beginning and end of a working day generally do not permit addressing matters that require discussion. These are better handled at regularly scheduled conferences. An exception would be a problem that cannot remain unresolved without either the nanny or parent feeling uncomfortable about it. In that event, an emergency conference would have to be requested.

A weekly or biweekly conference of a half-hour to one hour is usually sufficient to cover most matters. A commitment to set aside a special time to meet regularly attests to the importance the nanny and the parents attach to ongoing communications and their working relationship. When the lines of communication are kept open and there are opportunities to voice concerns, problems are likely to be discussed amicably and constructively, rather than getting to the point of "exploding" and seriously damaging the relationship.

Topics for discussion will vary from family to family and from week to week in the same family. The children's development and well-being are typically discussed at each conference. A review of the daily log can be helpful for this discussion. At various times, vacations, holidays, or special events may need to be scheduled, or there may be concerns about duties, hours, or other work-related matters. While problems should certainly be aired at conferences, nannies and employers should also use the time together to make positive comments as appropriate. Relationships prosper when appreciation and respect are communicated.

Longer conferences may be scheduled periodically as needed. For example, if a new baby is expected in the family, a discussion about how this might impact on the current work arrangements would be necessary so changes could be planned. Even without a significant event such as an additional child in the family, the nanny's job description should be reviewed every six months to determine if it is working satisfactorily for both the nanny and the employers, or if some changes are needed.

Conferences are more productive and use time more effectively if they are planned. Both the nanny and the parents need to know the topics to be discussed, particularly when the agenda is to include matters other than the sharing of routine information and concerns. When parents want to schedule an emergency or special conference, ask what their concerns are so you can be prepared for the conference. Similarly, when you ask to meet with parents about a particular matter, tell them what it is you wish to discuss. Regular weekly or biweekly conferences will be more efficient if a written format is followed so that all necessary points are covered and discussion remains focused.

JOB PERFORMANCE REVIEW

The job performance review is another example of maintaining good communication between the nanny and the employer. It provides an opportunity to discuss past performance and to plan future goals and accomplishments. It involves not only an evaluation of the nanny's performance by the employer, but also self-evaluation on the part of the nanny. If communication between the nanny and the employer is good, the performance review will hold no surprises, because work-related problems are addressed as they arise.

An informal review can be done at any time during regular parent/nanny conferences. It is a good idea for the nanny and employer to discuss how things are going several times during the first few weeks of employment and determine any need for change. A more formal evaluation, using a form to put it in writing, is usually done after six months of employment and every six months thereafter. A salary review, together with a review of the employment agreement including the nanny's job description, should be part of the formal review. A written commitment to provide the nanny with a written job performance review may be included in the written employment agreement. A suggested evaluation form appears in Appendix C.

The performance review should be approached as a learning experience and welcomed as an opportunity to grow professionally. Most of your performance as a nanny involves using the skills and attributes that earned you the job in the first place. Child-care skills and a professional attitude toward work are important to employers seeking a nanny and these are the areas that will be evaluated in the review. Criteria for evaluating job performance should correspond to the nanny's written job description.

Ask for a copy of the evaluation form to be used or offer to help develop one with your employer. Use the form to evaluate yourself in advance of your employer's review. Avoid being over-critical or too lenient with yourself. Keep in mind the compliments or criticism about your work that your employer may already have given you. Use your self-evaluation for building on your strengths and resolving to improve where necessary. Your perception of how you are doing should be part of your performance review with your employer and you need to be prepared.

In the event your employer rates you lower in a category than you think you deserve, keep calm and ask for more information. Suppose the issue is punctuality. Ask your employer to be specific. Be polite. This is not the time to point out angrily to employers that they often get home late and delay your going off duty. A reasonable discussion of the matter might convince your employer to upgrade your rating. Again, it must be emphasized that dealing with problems as they arise is best. If you have a concern about your employers' late arrivals home, raise it at the weekly conference. Similarly, employers should not hesitate to tell the nanny promptly if there is anything they are not satisfied with, so that improvement can be shown before the performance review. Use criticism as a way to learn what is important to your employer. Whether it is doing the baby's laundry on certain days, or organizing the playroom a particular way, comply with your employer's preferences.

GUIDELINES FOR EFFECTIVE COMMUNICATIONS

Communication is a complex process. To be successful, it requires effective expression of feelings and ideas, active listening, and attention to the nonverbal and emotional components of communication. It involves being aware that our attitudes toward other people are reflected in the way we communicate with them.

Good communication skills are essential to any professional situation. Nannies need to be attuned to their employers in order to provide the best possible professional service. They need to be able to deal with sensitive issues in open and constructive ways. The following guidelines offer practical suggestions for avoiding common pitfalls in communication and for using techniques that are effective.

Be Open and Honest about Your Concerns: Few things are more damaging to a relationship than the failure of one party to voice a concern so that the other party can be aware of it and have the opportunity to address it. There are several reasons why nannies may hesitate to be open and honest with employers. There may be the fear of losing a job if a criticism is aired. Age or **socioeconomic** differences between the nanny and the employers may make the nanny reluctant to express opinions. It may seem easier to resign from a position voluntarily rather than risk dismissal or try to improve the situation. Nevertheless, nannies have a professional obligation to be open and honest with the families they serve. Parents and nannies share the common goal of promoting the child's well-being. Good communications are vital to achieving this goal. The nanny may have to take the lead in making good communications the cornerstone of the nanny/employer relationship. Although nanny employers may be highly successful in their professional lives, it must not be assumed that they are at ease when talking about matters related to their children and home. Sometimes employers hesitate to voice criticisms or concerns because they are afraid of upsetting or losing the nanny.

Focus on Specific Concerns: It is difficult to grasp and address a problem if it is not described in a clear and specific way. Generalizations should be avoided. The implication that employers are unfair people or poor parents because of a particular situation will make them feel under attack and prevent frank, constructive discussion of the issue. Avoid exaggeration or placing blame. Statements such as "I never have time to myself" or "You just don't appreciate what I do for you" are not helpful in understanding and addressing a problem.

When you have an issue to raise, identify exactly what is troubling you in advance of talking to your employers. Whether it is your employers' frequent late arrivals home that result in your going off duty late, or a child who is too sleepy in them mornings to get ready for nursery school because of his late bedtime, consider the facts carefully and how you will present them clearly and calmly. Think of possible solutions to the problem and what compromises you would be willing to make. State the situation as you

---

socioeconomic—Involving both social and economic factors.

see it and use "I" statements. For example: "I am scheduled to work until six, but I find that I am having to stay until seven or later. How can we resolve this?" When the problem has been explained clearly and specifically, employers are in a position to consider it.

Be an Active Listener: An essential element in effective communications is actively listening to what the other person is saying. This involves attention to the entire message that is being sent and includes not only the words spoken but the tone of voice, the facial expression, posture, and hand movements of the speaker. This is called **body language** and much can be learned about the speaker's attitude and feelings by observing it. In active listening these observations are used to understand and interpret the deeper meaning of the message behind the words.

The active listener tries to listen objectively and avoids emotional reactions such as "You've got it all wrong," or "You can't really think that." Emotional reactions create barriers to communications. Instead, the active listener remains nonjudgmental and does not contribute new information to the discussion before hearing the other person out. Active listening prevents misunderstandings, keeps communications open, clarifies issues, and facilitates problem-solving.

Active listening usually does not come naturally. Most of us have learned to react to words instead of understanding the full message behind them. All too often, an answer forms in the mind and rises to the lips before the other person has finished speaking. It takes practice and a willingness to monitor one's current style of communicating to develop active listening skills.

Active listening helps nannies to understand parents' concerns about childrearing issues, being away from their children, or having their children in someone else's care. Use active listening skills to understand what parents expect from you with regard to the care of their children. Use these skills with children,

---

body language—Nonverbal communication unconsciously expressed in body movements, gestures, and facial expression.

too. By being an active listener, you encourage children to express their thoughts and feelings and discover their own solutions to problems.

BIBLIOGRAPHY

Bassett, M. (1995). *Infant and Child Care Skills*. Albany, NY: Delmar Publishers.

Charlesworth, E., and Nathan, R. (1984). *Stress Management*, Section V: Communicating Your Needs and Feelings. New York: Ballantine Books.

Counselman, K. (1989). "Honesty in the Nanny/Client Relationship." *National Nanny Newsletter* 5(3), 9.

Douville-Watson, L., and Watson, . (1988). *Family Actualization through Research and Education*, third edition. New York: Actualization, Inc.

Forney, D. (1990). "Can We Talk?" *National Nanny Newsletter* 6(1), 7.

Gordan, A., and Browne, K.W. (1993). *Beginnings and Beyond*, third edition. Albany, NY: Delmar Publishers.

Marston, S. (1990). *Nurturing Your Child's Self-Esteem*. New York: William Morrow and Company.

Rice, R. (1987). *The American Nanny*, revised and expanded edition. New York: Harper and Row, Publishers.

Steward, J., Editor (1990). *Bridges Not Walls*. New York: McGraw-Hill.

Chapter 6

Personal Health and Enrichment

TOPICS

- ◆ Introduction
- ◆ Maintaining a Healthy Lifestyle
- ◆ Good Posture and Body Mechanics
- ◆ Recreation

- ◆ Networking with Other Child-Care Professionals
- ◆ Dress, Grooming, and Wardrobe Planning
- ◆ Social Skills
- ◆ Travel

Terms to Know

health	*calorie*
burnout	*posture*
nutrition	*cardiovascular*
prenatal care	*body mechanics*
self-esteem	*etiquette*
hygiene	*courtesy*
stress	*visa*
nutrient	

INTRODUCTION

Good **health** and feeling confident in the many situations likely to be encountered in the course of employment are important aspects of being an effective nanny. Those in caretaking professions often overlook the need to take care of themselves, but it is essential in order to do the best job possible and avoid **burnout**. Working with young children and their families is physically and emotionally demanding. Nannies also need to provide children with positive role models in many aspects of everyday life. This chapter explores ways to promote the nanny's well-being and to prepare for the challenge of new experiences on the job. This information is not intended as a substitute for professional health care.

MAINTAINING A HEALTHY LIFESTYLE

Nannies owe it to their employers, the children they care for and, most of all, to themselves to strive for optimum health.

What Is Health?

Health is a state of physical, mental, and social well-being. Common factors influencing an individual's health include hered-

---

health—*State of physical, mental, and social well-being.*

burnout—*Exhaustion resulting from overwork and related* ***stress***.

ity, environment, **nutrition**, accidents, knowledge or ignorance of healthy practices, and access to medical care. It also includes **prenatal care** and care during childhood (a safe environment, nutrition, health practices conducive to cleanliness and adequate rest, a secure home life).

Components of Health

Regardless of age, state of health or disability, everyone has basic living needs. Meeting these needs adequately in ways appropriate to the individual is essential to maintaining a healthy lifestyle.

Personal Care and Hygiene: The daily shower or bath, freshly washed hair, clean teeth and nails, and clean clothing contribute to physical, mental, and social well-being. They make you look good and feel good and enhance **self-esteem**. Careful attention to **personal hygiene**, including frequent and proper handwashing, helps to protect the body from infection and control its spread.

Sleep and Rest: The amount of sleep and rest needed by an individual is determined by age, size, activities, and physical and mental condition. An average healthy adult requires eight hours of sleep balanced by 16 hours of activity each day. Sleep and rest refresh both the mind and the body. Inadequate sleep and rest

---

nutrition—*The study of food and how it is used by the body. Also, the sum total of the processes by which food is taken in and used by the body for survival, growth, and repair.*

prenatal care—*Medical supervision of a pregnant woman and the fetus.*

self-esteem—*How a person thinks and feels about himself or herself.*

personal hygiene—*Personal habits contributing to health, such as handwashing, bathing/showering, care of teeth, nails and hair, and wearing clean clothing.*

lead to fatigue and reduced ability to concentrate or manage **stress**.

Nutrition: Good nutrition is necessary for all parts of the body to function properly. Faulty diet and poor eating habits can lead to serious health problems. Good nutritional habits include a balanced diet, regular meals including breakfast, adequate time to eat and a pleasant mealtime environment. The food guide pyramid in Figure 6.1 suggests wise choices from each food group and how much is needed to obtain necessary **nutrients** without too many **calories** or too much fat, sugar, salt, or alcohol. Figure 6.2 explains what counts as a serving in each of the food groups. A healthy diet includes drinking six to eight glasses of water a day, in addition to food and other beverages.

Elimination: The body gets rid of waste products through the skin, kidneys, intestines, and lungs. Elimination is a regular, automatic function of a healthy body. It is influenced by diet, fluid intake, temperature, exercise, **posture**, and habits. Excitement, fear, anger, lack of privacy, pain, illness, and changes in daily routines can also affect elimination.

Exercise and Activity: Exercise is necessary for proper muscle tone and body function. The benefits of exercise are many and include muscular strength, increased stamina, improved posture, flexibility, **cardiovascular** endurance, leaner body composition, sense of well-being, and the ability to relax. Moderate levels of exercise are quite effective in controlling weight, reducing the risk

---

stress—*Tension in response to a physical, mental, or emotional demands on the body.*

nutrient—*Substance or component of food; has specific uses in the body.*

calorie—*Unit used to measure the energy value of food.*

posture—*Position of the body.*

cardiovascular—*Pertaining to the heart and blood vessels.*

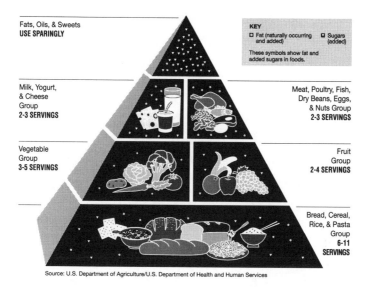

Figure 6.1 Food Guide Pyramid.
(Source: U.S. Department of Agriculture/U.S. Department of Health and Human Services)

of cardiovascular illness, and promoting overall fitness. An exercise program should be started slowly and a physician consulted first by those who are really out of shape. A realistic goal is 20 to 30 minutes of sustained activity three to five times a week. Brisk walking, dancing, bicycling, swimming, and skating are a few of the many activities that provide exercise and can be fun, too. Even climbing the stairs, washing and waxing a car, housework, and gardening provide exercise. Vigorous exercise should always begin with warming up to prevent injury and end with cooling down to bring the heartbeat back to normal gradually.

Environment: A clean, comfortable and safe environment promotes mental and physical health. A distressful environment can interrupt work, sleep, and relaxation. It can interfere with privacy and also lead to accidents. Fresh air is an important part of the environment because oxygen is essential to life. Fresh air ensures

What Counts as a Serving?

Food Groups:

Bread, Cereal, Rice, and Pasta

1 slice of bread	1 ounce of ready-to-eat cereal	1/2 cup of cooked cereal, rice or pasta

Vegetable

1 cup of raw leafy vegetables	1/2 cup of other vegetables, cooked or chopped raw	3/4 cup of vegetable juice

Fruit

1 medium apple, banana, orange	1/2 cup of chopped, cooked, or canned fruit	3/4 cup of fruit juice

Milk, Yogurt, and Cheese

1 cup of milk or yogurt	1-1/2 ounces of natural cheese	2 ounces of process cheese

Meat, Poultry, Fish, Dry Beans, Eggs, and Nuts

2–3 ounces of cooked lean meat, poultry, or fish	1/2 cup of cooked dry beans, 1 egg, or 2 tablespoons of peanut butter count as 1 ounce of lean meat

Figure 6.2   What counts as a serving?
(Source: U.S. Department of Agriculture/U.S. Department of Health and Human Services)

good ventilation of the lungs, encourages restful sleep, promotes general well-being, and helps prevent the spread of infection. A healthy lifestyle includes getting fresh air every day, even during cold weather.

Diversion and Recreation: Everyone needs a change from usual routines and pursuits in order to have a balanced and healthy life. A change from the routine refreshes the mind and body and can improve job performance. Recreational activities vary from person to person, depending on individual interests. Recreation for nannies is discussed in detail on pages 115–116.

Mental Well-Being: Mental well-being has to do with the way a person thinks, feels, behaves, and interacts. Physical and mental well-being influence each other. People who enjoy mental well-being are reasonably worry-free. They possess coping skills for dealing with the tensions and crises of life. They seek help when necessary. They take disappointments in their stride and accept criticism constructively. They make adjustments and decisions with relative ease. For them, life is generally enjoyable. They accept themselves and others and form satisfying relationships.

Preventive Health Care: Regular examinations by health professionals help to maintain good health and identify problems promptly. These include medical, dental, and eye examinations. Your own health professionals can suggest a schedule of regular checkups that is right for you. The health professional conducting the examination should be made aware of the nature and demands of the work you do.

Immunizations against communicable diseases should be maintained by those who care for young children. Any special concerns about exposure to illness while working with children and families should be discussed. Additional concerns may include weight control, an exercise program, prudent use of alcoholic beverages, how to stop smoking, or any other health matter of interest to the individual. Increased knowledge helps you take charge of your health and care for yourself better.

Safety: No discussion of a healthy lifestyle would be complete without mentioning safety. Accidents account for an enormous number of disabilities and deaths in the United States each year. Most accidents are the result of ignorance or carelessness and are preventable. Besides maintaining safe environments for children and providing good role models, nannies need to protect themselves from injury for their own well-being. Traffic laws must be obeyed, seat belts worn, and motor vehicles kept in sound operating condition. Recreational equipment must be kept in good working condition. Life jackets must be worn for water activities (e.g., boating, waterskiing) and swimming must never be done alone. Instructions for the proper use of products, equipment, and appliances must be carefully read and followed. Emergency plans in the event of fire, injury, sudden illness, or natural disaster must be established. Whether there are children in the home or not, safety precautions are needed to reduce risk of injury from falls, poisoning, heavy or sharp objects, and fire.

GOOD POSTURE AND BODY MECHANICS

Posture

Good posture contributes to physical well-being, prevents chronic and recurring discomfort and pain, and increases energy. It helps you project a positive, self-confident image. Clothes look better when you are "standing tall." Poor posture makes a person look out of shape and unsure. It causes muscle tension, stiffness, fatigue, backache, and even long-term injury. Given the physical demands of child care, good posture is extremely important for the nanny's well-being.

The goal of good posture is to keep the three natural curves of the spine in alignment. The three curves are the cervical curve of the neck, the thoracic curve of the middle back and the lumbar curve of the lower back. They are in good alignment when an imaginary straight line down the side of the body touches the ear, shoulder, pelvis, knee, and ankle bone. The chin should be parallel to the floor and not thrust forward. A stiff, military stance should be avoided and knees should not be locked. Abdominal muscles should be tightened to support the lower back. Awareness about how good posture feels helps you maintain it whatever you are doing. It allows for maximum comfort for sitting, standing, and walking.

To improve posture, evaluate how you sit and stand while doing various activities. Make a conscious effort to use good posture so it becomes a habit. Weight control and exercises to increase flexibility and strengthen lower abdominal muscles can improve posture (consult a physician for a safe, effective weight control or exercise program).

High-heeled shoes put strain on the lower back. Foot discomfort caused by ill-fitting shoes can also interfere with good posture. Shoes that conform to the natural shape of the foot, with low heels and good arch supports, provide comfort and help avoid injury (see page 119 for more information on selecting shoes).

Use chairs that allow you to sit straight with your feet supported, not dangling. Avoid crossing one leg over the other at the knee as this interferes with circulation. Get up and move around every half hour if you are sitting for a prolonged period. Adjust the car seat so you do not have to stretch your leg to reach the pedals while driving. A small cushion may be helpful in achieving a correct sitting position and providing support to the lower back. If you ride a bicycle, select one that does not require you to hunch over the handlebars. Sleep on your back or side on a firm mattress. Use only one pillow under your head.

Prolonged standing places strain on the lower back. A work area that is too high or too low can make the muscles of the neck and shoulders tense. Shift position as often as you can while standing. Take a break and move around whenever you can. Resting one foot on a low stool helps to support the lower back. Change feet periodically.

Avoid overloading handbags, shoulder bags, or diaper bags. Alternate the shoulder or arm you use to carry any bag or case. Choose bags that are lightweight when empty, so the bag itself does not add weight to your load. Consider using a knapsack-style bag that puts equal weight on both sides of the body when both straps are used (and keeps the nanny's hands free for other things such as holding the child's hand).

Body Mechanics

Good **body mechanics** are good posture in motion. Lifting, bending, and reaching must be done correctly to avoid back pain or injury. Since child care involves frequent lifting, it is essential

---

body mechanics—The various systems of the body working together to maintain balance and posture.

for nannies to use proper techniques. Whether you are lifting a child or an object, keep the following guidelines in mind:

- Always take time to think what you are doing and do it properly. No matter how busy you are, do not rush.

- Spread your feet slightly apart (about shoulder-width) for balance and a good base of support.

- Get close to the load or work area. Do not stretch to reach it. Draw the object close to you, keeping your arms and elbows close to your body to keep the weight centered.

- Tighten abdominal muscles.

- Bend your knees.

- Get a firm grip on the load using your whole hand.

- Lift with your legs, allowing powerful leg muscles to do the work rather than weaker back muscles.

- Maintain the natural curve of the spine; when bending, bend at the hips, not the waist.

- Avoid twisting the body while lifting. If turning is necessary while carrying a load, change the position of the feet toward the direction you want to move.

- Obtain help to lift anything that is too heavy or awkward for you to lift safely by yourself.

RECREATION

Everyone benefits from recreational activities that stimulate, relax, and refresh. This section considers the special demands of work as a nanny, the stress that may be experienced, and ideas for enjoyable recreational activities.

The Demands of Work in a Private Home

Thinking ahead of some of the special demands of a job helps with plans for dealing with them. Demands to consider in nanny employment include:

- The physical work involved in caring for young children.

- The emotional demands placed on those who work with children and their families.

- Getting along with parents, particularly when parents are under stress.

- The unique work setting, that is, the closeness and intimacy of the home.

- The isolation of in-home child care and lack of adult company while working.

- Adjustments to residing in another's home.

- Adjustments to differing opinions, values, and backgrounds.

- Being at a distance from family, friends, and familiar surroundings; coping with homesickness.

Stress

Stress is present at every stage of life. Without stress, life would lose much of its excitement, interest, and challenge. Stress keeps us alert, aware, and on our toes. Too much stress, though, can make a person miserable, sad, and exhausted, with serious consequences for physical and mental well-being.

Stress results from physical and mental or emotional activity. What is stressful for one person may not be stressful for another. Excessive stress may result from the building up of daily frustrations or from major changes or events in an individual's life. Changes or events do not have to be negative to be stressful. For example, starting a new and interesting job, marriage, a baby's birth, holidays, and vacations are usually perceived as occasions for happiness, but nevertheless can be stressful.

Recognizing the early signs of too much stress or distress is an important factor in coping with it successfully. Indications of harmful stress include a worried, uptight feeling, irritability, nervousness, trembling, dizziness, indigestion, loss of appetite or excessive eating, inability to slow down or relax, headache, backache, fatigue, reduced ability to enjoy life, and increased reliance on alcohol and other drugs. By becoming aware of your own individual response to stress, you will learn how to manage it in ways that are effective for you. Consider the following ideas:

- ◆ Daily exercise helps to relieve stress in an ongoing way and physical activity is an excellent remedy whenever you are upset, angry, nervous, or worried. Rather than sitting and fretting, it is much more helpful to go for a walk, play a vigorous game of tennis, or work in the garden ("And dig till you gently perspire," as Rudyard Kipling put it). The mind and body affect each other. Physical activity relieves tension, encourages relaxation, and helps you get a new perspective on whatever is troubling you.

- ◆ Take care of your health needs. Stressful situations will be more difficult to handle if you are already tired and irritable from insufficient sleep or inadequate nutrition.

- ◆ Plan your work so you use time and energy efficiently. Stress builds when tasks seem never ending.

- ◆ Set realistic goals for yourself. Expecting too much of yourself leads to disappointment and distress when things do not work out as you hoped.

- ◆ Recognize that there are some situations over which you have no control. Learn to accept what you cannot change.

- ◆ Share worries with a trusted friend or relative. Sometimes just talking about a problem helps you see it differently or arrive at a solution. For a serious problem, professional counseling may be necessary.

- ◆ If possible, avoid having too many significant changes in your life at one time.

- ◆ Never forget how to play and have fun. Make a commitment to do the things you enjoy. Make time in your schedule for recreational activities just as you do for work. Learn the art of relaxation (see Figure 6.3).

The best strategy for avoiding stress is to learn how to relax. Unfortunately, many people try to relax at the same pace that they lead the rest of their lives. For a while, tune out your worries about time, productivity, and "doing right." You will find satisfaction in just *being*, without striving. Find activities that give you pleasure and that are good for your mental and physical well-being. Forget about always winning. Focus on relaxation, enjoyment, and health. If the stress in your life seems insurmountable, you may find it beneficial to see a mental health counselor. *Be good to yourself.*

L.E. Koplow, M.D. (1983)

Figure 6.3 The Art of Relaxation.
(Source: U.S. Department of Health and Human Services, National Institute of Mental Health)

Recreational Opportunities

Finding interesting activities for off-duty hours needs to be approached in the spirit of adventure, especially for the nanny who has taken a position in a new community. Making an effort to identify recreational opportunities goes a long way toward settling into new surroundings, making new friends, and overcoming any homesickness that may be experienced. Try to achieve a balance with activities that satisfy social, intellectual, entertainment, fitness, educational, religious, service, and creative needs.

If you are new to an area, obtain a map and explore. Contact the local Chamber of Commerce for literature about interesting places, events, and organizations in the community. The public library and the local recreation department (usually part of the Board of Education) are also good sources of information about what is available in a community. They usually offer many programs of their own. Many communities have public swimming pools and some have ice-skating rinks. Softball or volleyball teams are other possibilities. The YMCA/YWCA may have fitness and other programs of interest. Adult education programs offer a wide range of courses that include fitness, learning a new creative skill or foreign language, cooking, computer skills, travel, writing, and much more. You may want to take a course at a community college, either for your personal enrichment or to improve job-related knowledge and skills. All of these kinds of activities offer opportunities for meeting new people and making friends, besides providing stimulation and a sense of accomplishment.

Joining the church, temple, or other religious institution of your choice is another good way to become involved in a community and meet people, as well as fulfill spiritual needs. Participation in the choir, social action, fund-raising events, potluck meals, teaching children, and study groups are among the many activities usually available at places of worship besides regular services.

Museums, concerts, theaters, parks, and zoological and botanical gardens are likely to be available in or near the metropolitan areas where many nannies work. There is usually a wealth of interesting things to do or see, whatever your taste or entertainment budget may be (it is possible to find many that are free).

Try to maintain any hobbies or talents that have given you pleasure in the past. Whether it is singing, playing a musical instrument, acting, painting, photography, baking, gardening, sports, or any other pursuit, find time to do what you enjoy.

Consider volunteering. It is a great way to overcome loneliness and boredom. Volunteers are usually needed by a wide range of organizations including hospitals, nursing homes, schools, and social service agencies.

Take time to read a book, walk in the woods, watch a sunset, and just enjoy a little peace and quiet every day. Balance stimulating activities with ones that are soothing.

NETWORKING WITH OTHER CHILD-CARE PROFESSIONALS

Getting involved with others in your chosen field of work has several benefits. It provides a source for support, information, and professional growth. It can also be fun to socialize with those who share the same interests, concerns, and experiences. It is especially helpful for nannies because they do not work with colleagues on a day-to-day basis.

National organizations for nannies and for those in the early childhood field in general are listed in Appendix D. Annual national conferences, newsletters, journals, educational materials, directories, and group health insurance are among the services such organizations may offer. A local chapter of a national organization may be available in your area, making it possible to attend nearby programs and workshops, participate in committee work and get to know other child-care professionals.

Nanny-organized support groups have been established in a number of cities in recent years. Offering professional programs and social events, these groups enable nannies to get to know other nannies in the neighborhood. Playgroups for nannies and children sometimes evolve, reducing the isolation felt by caring for children at home. To find out if there is a nanny support group near you, contact the National Association of Nannies (see Appendix D).

DRESS, GROOMING, AND WARDROBE PLANNING

An important part of a professional image is looking and feeling your best. It begins with the recognition that you are a unique and special person whose health and appearance are worth taking care of. By getting to know your own personal style and developing regular care routines, you project an image of self-confidence and a positive attitude.

Evaluate your current health habits and how you manage stress. Take a good look at yourself in a full-length mirror and check your posture, both sitting and standing. Resolve to make improvements where necessary. Taking care of your health is the foundation for an attractive appearance.

Personal Care

Daily care takes planning. Allow time for yourself every day. Rushing to get ready for work in the morning, relying on coffee for an energy boost, or going without breakfast are stressful ways to begin the day.

Hair should be neatly arranged and off the face for work. Choose a style that is easy to manage. A good haircut by a skillful stylist is a wise investment for both appearance and easy maintenance.

Caregivers of young children need to take special care of their hands. Good child care requires frequent, thorough handwashing, which dries the skin and may cause chapping. Use a mild soap and warm water, not hot, for washing hands. Dry thoroughly but gently. Apply lotion frequently during the day and at bedtime. Keep nails short. Nails should be trimmed and shaped weekly. If nail polish is worn, it must be renewed when it chips. Clear polish is preferred for work because it makes it easier to ensure nails are kept clean.

Cosmetics, perfume, and aftershave lotion should be used discreetly for work. Besides considerations of what is appropriate for the work setting, many personal care products have quite strong fragrances. A combination can be overpowering, or may provoke allergic reactions in sensitive individuals, particularly young children.

Wardrobe Planning

Clothes speak a powerful language. Although American nannies are usually not required to wear a uniform, their sense of professionalism can just as well be reflected in impeccable grooming and attire that is always neat, appropriate, and well-maintained.

Child care involves a lot of physical activity and careful attention to cleanliness. A nanny's everyday wardrobe must combine the need for comfortable, washable clothing with the need for a professional appearance. Besides home-based duties, the nanny is often out in the community on errands and outings or representing parents at the child's school, doctor's office, or friends' homes. Sweats, oversized or tight tee shirts, tee shirts bearing inappropriate messages, halter tops, bare midriffs, muscle shirts, and scanty shorts and skirts are not appropriate to the job. The formality of business attire is unnecessary for nannies. A classic casual look is more suitable for most occasions, but the nanny should also be prepared for events requiring more dressy or formal attire.

The mainstays of your wardrobe will probably be neat, washable slacks or skirts in basic colors, walking shorts for hot weather, and an assortment of coordinating blouses, shirts and sweaters. Waistbands that are partially elasticized allow for ease of movement.

Comfortable shoes are essential. They contribute to your well-being and help you to move around safely as you take care of children. Shoes made of leather allow moisture from sweat to escape and are more comfortable than synthetic materials. However, soles made of man-made materials are usually more flexible and less likely to be slippery than leather. Choose shoes that provide room to move the toes freely, grip the heel firmly, and are shaped like your own foot. Shoes should be comfortable the first time you try them on. A low-heeled leather walking shoe, with good support and in a basic color, is a good choice. Athletic shoes can be acceptable for everyday child-care duties provided they are kept clean (including laces) and replaced at first sign of shabbiness. For dressier occasions, women should avoid shoes with heels higher than two and one quarter inches. Apart from the discomfort or injuries that high heels may cause, they do not provide safe balance and support while handling children. Nannies are sometimes involved in family occasions requiring dressier clothes while caring for children. Fortunately, there are many attractively styled shoes available that are also practical.

General Guidelines for Selecting Clothes: Building a wardrobe that prepares you for everyday duties and special occasions at work need not be expensive. A wise principle to follow is to emphasize quality over quantity. One good item that makes you feel your best and wears well is a much better purchase than two items that do not fit or feel quite right and are not well-made. The best fabrics wash or dry clean successfully. When possible, choose natural fabrics such as cotton, wool or linen, or blends for easier maintenance and wearability. For dressier wear, silk is another option. Choose leather for shoes, belts, handbags, and gloves.

Plan before shopping. Review your existing wardrobe and decide what kinds of items you need to extend it. Consider the activities in which you are likely to be involved as a nanny. These may include not only direct child-care duties, but activities such as taking a child to swimming lessons or a children's concert, attending a family party, wedding, or funeral, dining out at a fine restaurant with your employers or accompanying them on a family trip. You may also attend conferences and meetings of professional associations to which you belong.

Your wardrobe planning will also be influenced by where your job is located. The prevailing climate, region of the country, and whether the job is in the city, suburbs, the country, or at the beach are factors to consider. Your employers' lifestyle is another factor. The family may be very formal, very relaxed and casual, or somewhere between. Do not hesitate to ask what your employers prefer you wear for work if you are uncertain.

Look at clothing catalogs and magazines for ideas. Several direct-merchant catalogs do, in fact, specialize in the type of classic casual, easy-care clothing that is appropriate for both men and women in child care.

Keep accessories simple for work. Avoid jewelry that has the potential to hurt a child, or may hurt you or be damaged if a child grabs it (e.g., rings with elaborate settings, dangling earrings, necklaces).

Once you have your shopping list, keep to it and resist impulse purchases. Make another list of items that you would like but are not essential and put them on your gift list for birthdays and other occasions.

Fit is an important factor in how clothes look and feel. Use a three-way mirror when trying clothes on. Make sure that once you have an outfit on, you can forget about it. Walk, sit, and bend to ensure that clothes will be comfortable and not need constant adjustment.

Guidelines for Women: Consider your personal style. Are you more comfortable in tailored clothes or in clothes with softer lines? Do you prefer a traditional look or a more creative one? Keep your silhouette in mind and choose lines that flatter you. Remember that tight clothing accentuates size rather than diminishes it. Choose colors that are becoming to you as well as practical. The secret of achieving a put-together look on a budget is to select a basic color for the major components of your wardrobe, usually black, navy, brown, or beige, and coordinate it with other colors that mix and match well. The following are suggested for your basic wardrobe:

- Full-length winter coat or all-season raincoat with zip-out lining (either of these should cover your longest skirt or dress).

- Casual jacket. Depending on climate, two may be needed— a heavy parka for winter and a lightweight, water-repellent jacket for other seasons.

- Slacks, skirts, and walking shorts.

- Coordinating long- and short-sleeved blouses, shirts, sweaters.

- Cardigan sweater.

- Dress. A classic style such as a shirtwaist, in your basic color or other medium to dark color such as royal, purple, or olive, can be used year-round and, with different accessories, be suitable for most occasions.

- Blazer to coordinate with slacks, skirts, dress.

- Suit (optional).

- Swimsuit.

- Underclothing, socks, pantyhose.

- Robe, sleepwear, slippers.

- Winter hat/cap and gloves to coordinate with winter outerwear.

- Leather walking shoes or athletic shoes for everyday.

- Shoes for dressier occasions, in basic color, heels no more than two and one quarter inches.

- Winter boots if climate requires them.

- Leather handbag in basic color.

- Scarves, belts, jewelry.

Guidelines for Men: The major items in a man's wardrobe, such as blazers and suits, tend to be more expensive than similar items for women. Nevertheless, it is wise to buy the best you can afford because such items can last for many years. Choose colors that you enjoy wearing for shirts and sweaters. Coordinate colors for slacks and shorts and invest in a good leather belt that goes with everything. Build a tie wardrobe with traditional designs and colors and with those that are more contemporary, according to your own preferences. The following are suggested for your basic wardrobe:

- All-season raincoat with zip-out lining.

- Casual jacket. Depending on climate, two may be needed— a heavy parka for winter and a lightweight, water-repellent jacket for other seasons.

- Washable slacks, walking shorts.

- Coordinating long- and short-sleeved shirts, sweaters.

- Blazer. Navy is a good choice. Teamed with gray dress slacks or good washable khakis and with a dress shirt and tie or a sport shirt, a navy blazer is useful for many occasions.

- Dress slacks to coordinate with blazer.

- Suit (optional). Dark gray or navy is a good choice.

- Dress shirt and ties to coordinate with blazer and suit.

- Swim trunks.

- Underclothing, socks (dress and athletic).

- Robe, sleepwear, slippers.

- Winter cap/hat and gloves to coordinate with winter outerwear.

- ◆ Leather walking shoes or athletic shoes for everyday.
- ◆ Dress shoes.
- ◆ Winter boots if climate requires them.
- ◆ Belts.

Wardrobe Maintenance

Regular care of clothing makes it last longer and helps to ensure that you always look your best. Schedule time every week to do laundry, ironing, any needed repairs, and shoe cleaning.

Organize your closet, drawers, and shelves so you can easily put an outfit together and not be in danger of forgetting what clothes you own. Use closet aids to keep clothes neat: padded hangers, hanging bars, slacks/skirt hangers, shoe bag or rack, clear plastic storage boxes, holders for belts, scarves, and ties.

Twice a year, usually in the spring and fall, reorganize your clothes. Discard any you know you will not wear again (many charitable organizations welcome used clothing in good condition) and identify any new items you need to buy or request as a gift. Wash or dry clean out-of-season clothes before storing. Protect stored woolens from moth damage.

Protect clothes with a clean apron when performing such tasks as bathing a baby or preparing food. Keep a spare set of clothes available at work in case clothing becomes soiled during child care. Clothes that are machine- or hand-washable are practical and keep dry-cleaning costs down.

Take time to read and follow the manufacturer's instructions for washing and drying. These are usually found on labels sewn in the garment. Save and use printed care instructions that come with shoes, boots, handbags, and some garments.

SOCIAL SKILLS

Social skills provide a nanny with the reassurance of knowing how to handle many different situations and demonstrate sensitivity to the feelings and comfort others.

Social skills or manners are necessary for group living. Whether the group is a family, a neighborhood, a region of the country, or a nation, the practice of social skills makes social interaction pleasant. Manners include rules of social behavior called **etiquette** which vary from one society to another and change as society changes. Most importantly, manners include unchanging rules that are rooted in ethics and values and are based on consideration and respect for others. The unchanging rules are expressed in **courtesy**. For example, table manners include certain conventions or etiquette with respect to the arrangement and use of each piece of flatware, how food is served and eaten, and where flatware should be placed at the conclusion of eating. Anyone who travels abroad quickly realizes that other countries do not observe exactly the same customs at mealtimes as the United States and that it is best to watch and follow those familiar with the customs. On the other hand, the rules that arise from the desire not to give offense while eating and to make mealtimes agreeable are more universal (Figure 6.4). These include the courtesy of coming to the table when called, serving others first, taking modest portions, eating quietly, not talking with a full mouth, keeping elbows to oneself, and saying "please" and "thank you."

The courteous person is nice to be around. Good manners are essential for positive relationships between nannies and employers and nannies and children. Courtesy is necessary for teaching children socially acceptable behavior. Modeling behavior that shows kindness and respect for everyone, including children, is the most effective way to raise a mannerly child.

There are almost endless ways to show a positive and thoughtful attitude toward others. Consider the following examples:

- ◆ Expressing thanks and appreciation of others, including thank-you letters written promptly.
- ◆ Responding to an invitation within a week of receiving it.

---

etiquette—*Rules of acceptable social behavior.*

courtesy—*Polite, gracious, and considerate behavior toward others.*

Figure 6.4 Knowledge of etiquette helps to smooth social interaction.
(Courtesy Murray State College, Tishomingo, Oklahoma)

- ◆ Not breaking a social engagement when a more attractive invitation for the same day arrives later.
- ◆ Letting others know in a timely way that you will not be at a meal for which you were expected.
- ◆ Being punctual; notifying others if you are delayed or plans change.
- ◆ Putting others at ease with introductions and conversation.
- ◆ Taking a genuine interest in the well-being of others.
- ◆ Apologizing to others for any hurt or inconvenience you may have caused.
- ◆ Listening to others with sincere interest and patience.
- ◆ Being considerate of other people's time; not talking too long (in person or on the telephone) or interrupting.
- ◆ Dealing with conflict calmly and with respect for differing points of view.

♦ Dealing with problems with the person concerned in private, not in the presence of others.

♦ Saying "No" without giving offense.

♦ Being cheerful and smiling, but never laughing at another person.

♦ Using a pleasant speaking voice.

♦ Offering a sincerely meant compliment.

♦ Speaking courteously to salespersons, restaurant staff, and anyone providing a service.

♦ Not disturbing the enjoyment and comfort of others in public places with loud voices or music or any kind of rowdiness.

♦ Observing silence at concerts, plays and movies, and in libraries.

♦ Taking your proper turn while waiting in line.

♦ Giving up a seat on public transportation to someone who is elderly, disabled, pregnant, or otherwise in greater need of a seat than you (for children this means giving up a seat for any adult).

♦ Holding doors open for those following you.

♦ Using good table manners and being attentive to the needs of others during meals.

♦ Taking telephone messages courteously and accurately (find out how your employer would like the telephone to be answered).

♦ Remaining calm and patient while driving; obeying the rules of the road (courteous driving is safe driving).

♦ Remembering that rudeness to children counts as rudeness; adults must be careful not to interrupt children, speak about them as if they were not present, or omit saying "please" and "thank you" to them.

Although good manners encompass much more than obeying a formal code of behavior, knowledge of etiquette helps to smooth social interaction and establish pleasant relationships. Practical etiquette that is useful for a nanny to know includes:

- How to set a table correctly for different kinds of meals.
- How to use flatware correctly.
- How to use a napkin correctly.
- Knowing the correct way to eat foods such as soup, asparagus, artichokes, shellfish, pasta, breads, and pastries.
- Appropriate manners in a restaurant.
- When and how much to tip.
- Selecting appropriate stationery for personal correspondence.
- When and how to write thank-you notes.
- How to respond to invitations.
- Addressing people properly.
- How to handle introductions when being introduced or introducing others.
- How to deal graciously with your employers' guests.
- Appropriate conduct when you are a guest in the homes of your employers' relatives and friends.
- Appropriate conduct for guests at celebrations such as weddings, christenings or dedications, confirmations, and Bar/Bat Mitzvahs.
- Appropriate conduct for funerals and memorial services; how to make a condolence call or write a letter of condolence.

An etiquette book can be a helpful addition to a nanny's library and suggestions will be found in Appendix E.

TRAVEL

As a nanny, you may have opportunities to travel. Whether it is in connection with interviewing for a position, attending a professional conference in another city, accompanying children and parents on trips, or your own vacation, being prepared and organized contributes to a successful trip and the avoidance of problems.

Travel needs to be approached with a sense of adventure whether it is work-related or for pleasure. Do not expect another country or another region of the United States to be the same as the place where you live. Seeing different people and being exposed to their culture, food, and environment can be an exciting opportunity for personal growth.

Before going on a trip, try to find out as much as possible about the places you will be visiting. Talk to those who have been there and ask about their favorite restaurants, hotels, stores, and places of interest. Inquire about the weather and the kind of clothes that local residents usually wear. Travel books from your public library can also provide information and tips for an enjoyable visit.

Making Travel Arrangements

The services of a travel agent can simplify purchasing airline tickets, making hotel reservations, renting a car, and dealing with other details of a trip. Although arrangements can be made directly with the companies involved, a travel agent is often aware of advantageous rates that an individual may have difficulty in discovering and can help plan the most convenient itinerary. A travel agent can assist in making arrangements that match individual needs and preferences and provide information about places to be visited. Recommendations from relatives, friends, and colleagues are the best way to begin the search for a reliable travel agent. To get the best services from an agent, it is important to be as specific as possible about the type of trip you have in mind and share any special requirements you may have. Although agents rely mostly on commissions from the companies with which they make bookings, determine in advance whether any fees for the agent's services are payable by the client.

Clothing for Travel

Plan clothing and other travel items carefully so you will be comfortable, relaxed, and have everything you need. Before packing, check a national newspaper for current weather in the cities you will visit or be near. For changeable weather, take clothing that can be layered as temperatures go up or down. Always be prepared for rain. Comfortable shoes are essential for any trip. Clothing choices will also be influenced by what you expect to be doing. A month by the ocean with your employing family will require different clothes from those suited to four days in a major city for a professional conference. Be sensitive to local customs when traveling abroad. In some countries, for example, it is unacceptable for a woman to display bare shoulders or arms in public.

For the journey, choose clothes that are comfortable, but also presentable. You will want to arrive looking professional and well-groomed. Cotton-knit fabrics are practical. They are suited to all seasons, resist wrinkles, and provide ease. Medium to dark colors show soil less quickly than pastels. Shoes provide better protection for the feet than sandals. Always have a sweater available for the journey. Air conditioning and fatigue can cause chilling.

Make a list of everything you will need. Keep your list. It can serve as an inventory in the event your luggage is lost and you need to file a claim. Travel as lightly as possible. Avoid taking any item of clothing that will be worn only once. Take clothes that will mix and match to create a variety of outfits. Plan a color scheme so that shoes and items such as a blazer, jacket, or sweater go with everything. Choose fabrics that are wrinkle-resistant and will not easily show dirt. Keep in mind the length of your stay and the availability of laundry facilities when you are deciding how much to take.

Packing

Items for the journey should be separated from items that will not be needed until the destination. For example, pack a small overnight bag that can easily be reached if you are traveling by car and a stop at a motel is planned en route. By plane, a change of clothing and basic toilet articles should be packed in the carry-on bag in the event checked-in luggage is delayed or lost. Other items to carry for your comfort during your flight or airport delays include a sweater, reading material, a nonperishable snack and bottled water (place in a sealable plastic bag in case it leaks), tissue, individually wrapped moist towelettes, and gum or hard candy to relieve ear pressure during takeoff and landing.

Airlines advise that medication, jewelry, keys, tickets and other travel documents, money, eyeglasses, cameras, and any other valuables should be carried. Have any telephone numbers or directions needed at your destination easily available. Air passengers are usually limited to one carry-on bag each. Keep it a manageable size because if it does not fit under the seat in front of you, it will have to go in the overhead storage bin where it will be less accessible. Also, anything not checked in has to be carried through airports and cannot be left unattended.

Methodical packing results in the minimum of wrinkled clothing, uses luggage space effectively, and reduces the possibility of forgetting something. Assemble all items to be packed on a bed or table. Check items on your list as you gather them. Make sure all clothing is clean and in good repair.

Place heavier items, such as shoes, by the hinges of a suitcase or at the bottom of a bag. Use soft fabric shoe bags to prevent shoes from getting scratched or clothes soiled (plastic bags may be used, but the shoes should not be wrapped airtight because condensation may form and spoil the leather). Use toe spaces in shoes for packing socks and other small items. Fill small spaces in the luggage with rolled up socks and underwear and similar items. Empty pockets, close zippers, and fasten buttons on shirts, blouses, and dresses. Fold clothes neatly and place in luggage in layers, as evenly as possible. Pack firmly so luggage contents do not move around, but do not overpack.

Avoid packing anything that is breakable. Take toiletries in unbreakable containers with caps securely fastened. Place them in sealable plastic bags for extra protection of clothes. Variations in temperature and pressure on an airplane can cause leakage. Take small sizes of items such as shampoo, lotion, and toothpaste to save space and weight.

Include a bag for soiled laundry. Other useful items include: small sewing kit, safety pins, powdered spot remover, travel clothesline and pins, travel alarm clock, small flashlight, night light, can/bottle opener, and a hairdryer (for travel abroad, an adapter is needed for this or any other appliance, such as an electric razor). If you wear contact lenses, remember to take needed equipment and solutions. Spare eyeglasses are a wise precaution. It is advisable to take your own washcloths for overseas travel, since these are not always provided in smaller hotels, bed-and-breakfast accommodations, or private homes. Taking soap is also advisable.

Certain items are prohibited on airplanes. Regulations that come with tickets should be read and followed. All carry-on luggage is subject to inspection at the security checkpoint.

Luggage should be labeled both inside and out. All luggage going by air is required to be labeled, whether checked or carried on board. On the outside, use labels that conceal your name and address from casual view. Remove old destination tags from your luggage for each new trip. When you claim your luggage at the end of the journey, check the claim check number and your name label to make sure it is yours.

Checked luggage should be locked. Luggage usually comes with duplicate keys that should be carried in separate places.

Tickets and Travel Documents

Tickets should be kept where they can easily be reached when they are required to be shown. If you have an itinerary showing flight numbers and departure and arrival times, keep it handy for easy reference. You will need your driver's license or another form of official identification when you are checking in for air travel. A driver's license is, of course, necessary if you plan to drive during the trip. A U.S. driver's license usually satisfies legal driving requirements in other countries.

Take confirmation slips/numbers with you for any hotel and car rental reservations you have made in advance.

If you are traveling abroad, a passport and possibly a **visa** will be necessary (see following section).

Passports and Visas

With the exception of Canada, Mexico, and some countries in Central and South America and the Caribbean, all United States citizens, including infants and children, need a valid passport to leave and return to the United States and to enter a foreign country. Even if your destination does not require a valid passport, some proof of United States citizenship or permanent residence may be needed to return to the United States. To be certain about requirements, always check before making travel plans. An informative pamphlet, "Foreign Entry Requirements," may be obtained from the United States Department of State, Bureau of Consular Affairs, Washington, DC 20520-4818. This includes information about visa requirements for some countries (see page 133). Questions may be directed to the Department of State by telephone at (202) 647-1488, to the office of your Congressional Representative or United States Senator, or to your travel agent.

First-time applicants for a passport must apply in person if they are 13 years or older. Applications may be made at selected post offices, regional passport agencies located in Boston, Chicago, Honolulu, Houston, Los Angeles, Miami, New Orleans, New York, Philadelphia, San Francisco, Seattle, Stamford, and Washington, DC, or with clerks of state and federal courts. The application form (DSP-11) provides complete information about the application procedure, including the documents, photographs, and fees that will be required when the application is submitted. Passports for those over 18 years are valid for 10 years and for those under 18 years, for five years.

Passports may be renewed by mail if you have your most recent passport and it was issued less than 12 years ago when you were 18 years or older. If your name is different from the one on the passport, you must be able to submit documentation of a

---

visa—*An endorsement on a passport authorizing entry into a particular country.*

name change by marriage or court order. The form for passport application by mail (DSP-82) provides complete instructions for the application procedure.

Allow several weeks to obtain a passport. Avoid applying just before travel is at its peak during the spring and summer months. Passports can be expedited when there is need to travel in three weeks or sooner. An additional fee and proof of departure date are necessary. Passports may be expedited at one of the regional passport agencies (see above). The office of your Congressional representative or United States senator can also assist with this process. Alternatively, particularly for a real emergency, the duty officer at the United States Department of State may be contacted at (202) 647-6633, or at (202) 647-4000 after business hours or at weekends. Any nanny who expects to travel abroad should consider obtaining a passport before the need arises.

Some foreign countries require a visa for entry in addition to a passport. Since the visa application process requires a valid passport and can itself be lengthy, careful advance planning is essential. Rules of entry vary from one country to another and may change suddenly. It is advisable to check on any country to be visited. Information may be obtained from regional passport agencies, offices of Congressional representatives and United States senators, and the United States Department of State (see page 132 for how to contact the Department of State and obtain a copy of "Foreign Entry Requirements"). A travel agent may be able to obtain a visa for you.

Money While Traveling

The use of credit cards, money cards, and personal and traveler's checks limits the amount of cash that needs to be carried around while traveling. Different businesses have their own policies about which forms of payment they will accept. Having several ways to pay at your disposal means, for example, that if traveler's checks are not accepted somewhere, you can use a credit card or personal check. It is advisable to find out in advance how payment may be made for such expenses as hotels, restaurants, entertainment, transportation, and large purchases at stores.

Traveler's checks may be purchased from a bank or through your travel agent. They may be purchased in United States dollars or in the currency of another country. Traveler's checks in United States dollars may be cashed in a bank in another country at the current rate of exchange (a foreign bank usually charges a commission fee). At home and abroad, identification is generally required to cash traveler's checks or make a purchase with them. Keep a list of each check's serial number separate from the checks themselves and record each check that is used. It is wise to leave another copy of the serial numbers with a friend or relative at home. In the event you need to report lost or stolen checks, the serial numbers are necessary. Traveler's checks should be treated like cash and guarded against loss or theft.

Major credit cards are accepted in many places abroad. Money cards provide a convenient way to obtain cash in a foreign country's currency. Contact the bank that issued your credit and money cards to determine if they can be used where you are going. Your bank can assist with any money-related questions you may have regarding travel in the United States and abroad.

United States Customs

For information about United States Customs regulations and requirements for those returning to the United States, an informative booklet, "Know Before You Go," is available (Department of the Treasury, U.S. Customs Service, Publication No. 512). A travel agent may be able to provide a copy.

Safety

Sensible precautions minimize the possibility of problems while traveling. In an unfamiliar environment, in the United States or abroad, travelers may be exposed to unexpected dangers or difficult situations. Tourists tend to be conspicuous and may be easy targets for thieves. Thinking ahead and exercising prudence helps to ensure a safe, enjoyable trip.

Leave expensive jewelry and watches at home. Clear your wallet of credit cards and other items not needed on the trip. Men should carry a wallet that is as slim as possible. Nothing valuable should be kept in a rear pants pocket even if it has a button. It is harder for a pickpocket to remove a wallet if it has rubber bands around it. Women should keep a wallet in a zippered compartment of a sturdy bag. The bag should be kept closed and held firmly. Be aware that pickpockets and bag-snatchers often work in pairs. One distracts the intended victim by asking a question or creating an incident while the other steals the wallet or purse.

Travelers are especially vulnerable to theft in air, train, and bus terminals, and for the first day in a new place. It is easy to be distracted in such situations, but extra alertness and care are needed. Never leave luggage and other belongings unattended.

When traveling by car, luggage and other items of value should be concealed from view in a locked trunk when the car is parked.

Avoid carrying all your money, credit cards, tickets, traveler's checks, and passport in one place. Use a hotel safe to store valuables you are not carrying. Carry only enough cash for one day. Keep the rest in traveler's checks or checks, or use a money card to withdraw only what you need. Remain extra alert and cautious when you are using an ATM machine, putting items in or taking them out of a safe or locker, or have your wallet or handbag open for a transaction.

In addition to keeping a record of traveler's check serial numbers (see page 134), make a copy of your credit cards, tickets, and passport and keep them separate from the originals (or exchange copies with the person you are traveling with). In the event of theft or loss, this information helps to protect accounts and obtain replacements.

Determine if you have insurance coverage for losses, medical emergencies, and driving while traveling, especially abroad where your usual coverage may not apply.

Use common sense about avoiding unsafe parts of a city or elsewhere, just as you would in your familiar surroundings. A hotel concierge can provide guidance about where to go and what to see and do. Most cities of any size that attract tourists in the United States and abroad have a tourist information center.

Centers offer information and advice on lodging, restaurants, entertainment, places of interest, and other matters of concern to tourists.

Pay attention to the safety instruction given on planes prior to take off. Identify exits and escape routes upon arrival in unfamiliar buildings such as hotels, theaters, and private homes. Be aware that if there is a fire or other emergency, evacuation may take place in the dark.

Keep your hotel door locked when you are in the room and when you are away. Do not open the door to anyone you are not expecting and do not know (call the front desk if you are uncertain about someone claiming to be hotel staff).

In the event of a problem abroad, such as a crime, lost passport or traveler's checks, or the need for an English-speaking physician, the United States Embassy or nearest consulate may be contacted for assistance. The United States Bureau of Consular Affairs issues brochures on travel to specific areas of the world including Mexico and the Caribbean. For more information about available brochures or to order (at $1 per brochure), contact the Superintendent of Documents, U.S. Government Printing Office, Washington, DC 20402, telephone (202) 783-3238. The Bureau issues additional helpful pamphlets including "A Safe Trip Abroad," "Your Trip Abroad," and "Tips for Americans Residing Abroad." These pamphlets are also available from the Government Printing Office for a modest charge. Take time to read the tips for travelers and other important information in your U.S. passport.

Health

Any medical, dental, or eye examinations that are coming due before a trip should be done in sufficient time for problems to be addressed. This is especially advisable before a trip abroad.

Planning for a healthy trip includes assuring an adequate supply of any medication taken regularly, extra eyeglasses or lens prescription, and an identification card or bracelet for anyone who has allergies or a medical condition that may need emergency care. Matters to be discussed with the physician may include motion sickness and travel to high altitudes (which may produce altitude sickness).

The physician or local health department can be sources of information about any health requirements of foreign countries to be visited. If immunizations are necessary, they should be done enough in advance so that a reaction will not interfere with comfort on the trip. Prescription medications should be carried in their original containers for trips abroad to avoid disputes with customs officials. A letter from the physician stating major health problems and dosages of prescribed medication is advisable in case emergency care is needed and to present to customs if necessary.

Diarrhea may be a problem while traveling, especially abroad. It may not be the case that water and food are contaminated, but that they are different from home. The physician should be asked about precautions to take to avoid diarrhea and remedies to pack in the event it occurs.

Where water is contaminated, ice cubes must be considered contaminated also. Containers that have held water or ice may also be contaminated, so drinking beverages directly from a can or bottle may be safer. When food safety is questionable, avoid raw or lightly cooked foods. Choose well-cooked dishes served hot and fruits with peel you remove yourself. Swimming in contaminated water may result in infections. If insects are a problem, wear protective clothing and use repellent. Some insects transmit illnesses from one person to another.

Moderation in eating, drinking, and activities is advisable for any travel. A first-aid kit and any needed medications should be packed where they can be reached during the journey. Allow for frequent stops for exercise and refreshments during car travel. When traveling by air, get up periodically and stretch the legs during a long flight. Eat lightly but maintain liquid intake. When traveling through several time zones, be prepared to adjust gradually over several days.

Common sense, planning, and the advice of your personal physician go a long way toward a healthy and enjoyable trip.

Travel with children involves additional planning and attention to safety and health not covered here (see child-care books listed in Appendix E).

BIBLIOGRAPHY

American Academy of Orthopedic Surgeons (1995). *If the Shoe Fits Wear It—Steps to Proper Shoe Fit* (brochure). Rosemont, IL: American Academy of Orthopedic Surgeons.

American Academy of Orthopedic Surgeons (1993). *Lift It Safe!* (brochure). Rosemont, IL: American Academy of Orthopedic Surgeons.

American Medical Women's Association (1995). *The Women's Complete Health Book*. New York: Delacorte Press.

Baldridge, L. (1990). *Manners for the '90s*. New York: Rawson Associates.

Changing Times (1986). "Tips for Troublefree Travel Abroad." *Changing Times*, May 1986, 45–46.

Charlesworth, E., and Nathan, R. (1984). *Stress Management*. New York: Ballantine Books.

Chase, D. (1989). *The New Medically Based No-Nonsense Beauty Book*. New York, Henry Holt and Company.

Coffey, Barbara, and the Editors of Glamour (1979). *Glamour's Success Book*. New York: Simon and Schuster.

Graber, E., and Siegel, P. (1990). *Fieldings Travelers Medical Companion*. New York: William Morrow and Company.

Grimes, P. (1985). *The New York Times Practical Traveler*. New York: Times Books.

Heloise (1985). *Heloise's Beauty Book*. New York: Arbor House.

Kendrick, S.K., Kaufman, R., and Messenger, K.P. (1995). *Healthy Young Children: A Manual for Programs*, Chapter 10, Adult Health. Washington, DC: National Association for the Education of Young Children.

Koplow, L.E. (1983). *Plain Talk About Handling Stress* (revised). United States Department of Health and Human Services

Publication No. (ADM)91-502 (reprinted 1991). Washington, DC: U.S. Government Printing Office.

Krames Communications (1986). *Poor Posture Hurts* (booklet). Daly City, CA: Krames Communications.

Prevention Magazine Health Books (1988). *Everyday Health Tips.* Emmaus, PA: Rodale Press.

United States Department of Agriculture (1992). *Food Guide Pyramid* (booklet HG-249). Hyattsville, MD: USDA-Human Nutrition Service.

Chapter 7

Preparing for Employment

TOPICS

- ◆ Introduction
- ◆ Types of Nanny Positions
- ◆ Sources of Nanny Employment
- ◆ Terms of Employment
- ◆ Taxes and Insurance

- ◆ Length of Commitment
- ◆ Contents of the Written Employment Agreement
- ◆ Job Application Requirements

Terms to Know

perquisite   *bonus*

gross salary   *contract*

INTRODUCTION

Selecting an employment situation that is likely to be professionally and personally satisfying can be a daunting task. Because each family is unique, each nanny position is unique. There are many factors to consider when deciding which job opportunities to pursue. A methodical, informed approach is necessary to reach a rational decision. It involves defining your job interests and requirements prior to exploring available positions. It requires making a distinction between the factors in a job that are essential to you and those for which you can be flexible. The rights and responsibilities of both the nanny and employer in an employment agreement must be understood. This chapter provides guidelines for approaching the process of seeking a job in an organized, knowledgeable way.

TYPES OF NANNY POSITIONS

Deciding whether to seek a live-in or live-out position is a major issue for some nannies. Maintaining one's own apartment has its appeal in terms of independence from the work setting during off-duty hours. On the other hand, it carries the responsibility of meeting expenses for rent, utilities, food and other costs, requires reliable transportation for traveling to and from work and lengthens the nanny's day because of travel time. A live-in nanny has room and board provided by the employer. A car, opportunities to travel with the family, and other **perquisites** are usually more common in live-in positions. Live-in nannies do not have to cope with rush-hour traffic or bad

---

perquisite—An extra benefit or privilege accompanying a job. Sometimes referred to colloquially as a perk.

weather in order to get to work. For some nannies, though, a live-in position may feel too restrictive. For nannies who already have their own homes, a live-out position with reasonable travel time is an obvious choice.

The decision to work full-time or part-time usually depends on factors in the nanny's personal life. Part-time employment may suit nannies with families of their own, for example.

Although many nanny positions are long-term, temporary situations do occur. An illness or another emergency in a family can create a need for a temporary nanny. Parents who do not normally employ a nanny may require one when they take a trip without the children. Some nannies specialize in newborn care and go from one family to another just for the first few weeks of the baby's life.

Location is another consideration. Jobs may be local, out-of-town, out-of-state, and occasionally abroad. They are most likely to be in or close to major metropolitan areas, although opportunities in rural or wilderness areas sometimes occur. A nanny who wants to relocate, perhaps to another part of the country, must be ready to adjust to an environment that may be very different from the familiar one. If you have not moved away from home before, relocating to a place you have already visited or where you have relatives or friends may be preferable. A nanny who prefers to work closer to home must be realistic about job availability. Nanny jobs may be rare or nonexistent in small towns away from a city of any size. A nanny must be willing to seek employment where it is available, just as in any other occupation.

Many other factors influence job preferences and may include: the children's ages, how many children, children with special needs, single-parent families, families where one parent stays at home, size of the household and whether it is formal or informal, religious preference of employers, travel opportunities, and pets. A household with two nannies is another type of situation that occurs from time to time.

Salary, benefits, and related job considerations are discussed later in this chapter.

SOURCES OF NANNY EMPLOYMENT

Nanny Placement Agencies

Agencies specializing in nanny placement are available in most cities throughout the United States. Licensing of nanny placement agencies is only required in some states and the industry is not uniformly regulated. It is therefore important to select an agency with care to ensure that you will get the services needed to find an appropriate position. The recommendation of other nannies who have used any agency you are considering is a good place to begin. Find out how long the agency has been in business and what professional qualifications the agency staff possesses for evaluating their family clients and being responsive to the employment interests of nannies.

An agency charges a fee to the family when a placement is made and sometimes for being registered with the agency. Usually no fee is charged to the nanny, but you should make sure of this before any services are provided. Obtain written information about any applicable fees and the services that the agency provides to the nanny before and after the placement, including the agency's obligation to the nanny if the placement is unsuccessful.

Find out how much information about prospective employers and the nanny position will be available to you. A responsible agency provides complete and accurate information about the nanny's duties, hours, salary, benefits, and other details relevant to the job. A description of the family as it relates to nanny employment is also provided, together with family references. Ask if other family screening is done besides references.

Before work begins, the agency should help the nanny to develop a written employment agreement that accurately reflects the arrangements made by the nanny and the employer.

A reputable agency will not approach you about job opportunities when you are already employed, unless you ask for assistance with finding another position.

Some nanny training programs offer their graduates placement assistance through their own placement service or agency.

Do not allow yourself to be pressured into interviewing for jobs in which you have no interest or accepting a job you do not want. When you do agree to an interview, keep the appointment that has been arranged and follow the agency's instructions for keeping in touch about the outcome.

Help Wanted Advertisements

Some employers prefer to advertise a nanny position in a newspaper instead of using a nanny placement agency. Look in newspapers with national circulation for jobs in various regions of the country and in local newspapers for local jobs. You will have to screen the advertising family carefully and be well-organized to obtain all the information you need to make a decision. Be aware that although a job may be advertised as a nanny position, it may really be for a babysitter or housekeeper. If you accept a position through these means, you will not have the assistance of an agency with a written employment agreement or support if problems arise.

Position Wanted Advertisement

You may decide to place an advertisement in a newspaper yourself. Careful screening of respondents will be necessary before you decide which families to meet for an interview. Again, it will be up to you to obtain all needed information to make a job decision, develop a written employment agreement, and deal with any problems without an agency's support.

Word of Mouth

The availability of good nannies or good job openings may be passed around by word of mouth among other nannies, friends, relatives, and employers. Keep in mind, though, that the job that suits one nanny may not suit another as well. Careful research and consideration of all relevant information is always necessary before committing to a job. Relatives or friends who want to put you in touch with someone in need of child care may not fully understand the nanny profession. Beware of any situation where your relationship with the prospective employer is too close for you to maintain professional distance and deal with problems objectively.

TERMS OF EMPLOYMENT

Job opportunities cannot be evaluated properly without knowing what is typically included in the nanny's job description and the compensation that may be reasonably expected. As a professional, a nanny should be aware of the duties that are usually expected and the value of the work performed. At the same time, it must be emphasized that no two nanny jobs are identical and careful consideration of all aspects of a position is necessary.

Nanny Job Description

A job description outlines the duties of a particular nanny position and should be prepared by the employer before interviewing candidates. In practice, this is not always done. Employers who are new to employing a nanny may have only a vague idea of what duties are appropriate to a nanny and need assistance in developing a realistic job description agreeable to them and the nanny.

When a job description has been established, it becomes part of the written employment agreement and should only be changed if the nanny and employer both agree. The trial period is a good time to see how the job description is working and adjust it if necessary. Changes are necessary when changes in the employing family occur, for example, when a new baby arrives, an older child begins school, or an employer's hours of work change. The job description can be changed at any time the nanny and employer agree that it is not serving its purpose well.

A nanny should not begin work without having the responsibilities of the job in writing. Without a job description, a nanny has no recourse if duties are changed or increased, or if claims are made that job responsibilities are not being met. Employers and nannies who enjoy a good working relationship seldom need to refer to the job description, but if a dispute arises, it is essential for addressing problems fairly and for protecting the nanny's professional reputation.

A job description cannot cover everything, but it should be sufficiently detailed to avoid misunderstanding and contribute to a harmonious working relationship. An example of a job description's inclusion in a written employment agreement appears in Appendix A.

In general, a nanny is employed by a private family on a live-in or live-out basis, to care for all young children in the home and to undertake housekeeping tasks related to child care. A full-time nanny usually works 45 to 60 hours per week, with two consecutive days off. The contents of a job description usually include but are not limited to the following areas:

Child care: Child's physical, emotional, social and intellectual development and well-being. Responsibilities usually include maintaining a safe, healthy and nurturing environment, using guidance and discipline according to parental preferences, planning and providing a balance of developmentally appropriate activities daily, planning and preparing nutritious meals and snacks for the child, and promoting stability and security in the child's life (Figure 7.1). Other specified responsibilities may include care of the sick child, care for the child while traveling, supervising homework and coordinating home and school learning time, and tutoring.

Household tasks: Children's laundry and mending; organization of children's clothing, toys, and other effects; cleaning and maintenance of the child's quarters and equipment; food preparation and clean-up for the child; and child-related errands, shopping, and transportation. Care and cleaning of the nanny's quarters, if applicable.

Reports to parents: Regular communications with parents about their child's health, development, and any special problems with daily logs, verbal reports, and conferences.

Figure 7.1 A nanny's job description includes planning and implementing healthy routines and developmentally appropriate activities.

Working/living relationships: Positive, cheerful attitude on duty and respect for the needs of the other household members for privacy and support.

Hours on duty: Up to 60 hours per week, scheduled to cover the time when child care is needed, for example:

◆ 7:30 AM to 6:30 PM Monday through Friday.

◆ Occasional 24-hour or evening coverage by arrangement.

Family needs for child-care coverage are so individual that there is no typical arrangement. However, a burnt-out nanny is not in anyone's interest. Additional hours should only be occasional and arranged in advance by mutual agreement. The nanny should have the option to decline as well as accept opportunities for additional hours.

Normally, nannies work during daytime hours, but there may be circumstances when this would not be the case, at least temporarily. Hours on duty are likely to be different when the nanny accompanies the family on a trip. In this case, hours should be discussed in advance so that parents have the coverage they need and the nanny also has time off. In a live-in situation where there is a newborn, the nanny might be on call for night feedings so the mother can get the rest needed after childbirth. A nanny should also be willing to offer reasonable flexibility with hours for family emergencies.

In a household where two nannies are employed, evening hours and being on call at night may alternate with daytime hours of duty.

Compensation

Salary, benefits, and other tangible rewards are considerations in any job. Compensation needs to be considered with the job description, the number of working hours, and any other aspect of nanny employment which you have identified as important to you.

Salary: Under the Fair Labor Standards Act (FLSA), nannies are entitled to be paid at least the FLSA minimum hourly rate of $5.15 (the rate effective September 1, 1997). This applies to both live-in and live-out nannies. Where state law requires a higher minimum wage, the higher standard applies. Additionally, in a live-out situation, the FLSA entitles the nanny to overtime at the rate of not less than one and one-half the regular pay rate for all hours in excess of 40 in a workweek. Employers are required to keep records of wages, hours, and other items specified in the U.S. Department of Labor recordkeeping regulations. Major provisions of the FLSA are summarized in a free booklet, "Handy Reference Guide to the Fair Labor Standards Act." Information specific to nanny employment is contained in "Regulations Part

552: Application of the Fair Labor Standards Act to Domestic Service." These publications are obtainable from the U.S. Department of Labor, Employment Standards Administration, Wage and Hour Division, Washington, DC 20210. Questions or requests for publications may also be directed to local Department of Labor offices.

Several factors may influence salary. Whether the position is live-in or live out can make a difference. Salary for a live-out position is generally higher because live-out nannies pay their own living expenses. The employer provides room and board for the live-in nanny, although this does not count as salary and is not taxable. The location of the job, benefits provided, nanny qualifications, and anything especially challenging about the job (such as young twins or triplets, or a child with a developmental or health problem requiring special care) may also make a difference. A 1996 survey of nannies conducted by the International Nanny Association indicated that **gross salaries** ranged from $175 per week to $450 or more. In 1995, a survey conducted by *Nanny News* reported an average hourly rate of $7.10.

The nanny's salary, together with job performance, should be reviewed after the first six months of work. It is not unusual for the written employment agreement to stipulate a raise at this time. Thereafter, a salary review occurs every six months or yearly, or at any time a change in the nanny's hours or responsibilities suggests a review would be appropriate. Raises are usually in the range of five to ten percent of the nanny's present salary. **Bonuses** may be offered by some employers instead of six-monthly salary raises. This may take the form of a cash percentage of the nanny's salary, a round-trip ticket home for the holidays, additional paid days off, or other rewards appropriate to the individual nanny and job situation.

Overtime pay is typically calculated at one and one half times the hourly rate. Arrangements must comply with FLSA requirements for domestic service employees.

---

gross salary—*Total of salary before deductions.*

bonus—*Payment or other reward given an employee over and above regular compensation.*

Room and Board: A private bedroom and bathroom are preferred minimum accommodations (sometimes the nanny is asked to share a bathroom with the children). Accommodations vary from one nanny position to another. A sitting room, a kitchenette, or an apartment with a separate entrance add to the nanny's comfort and privacy. Occasionally, housing arrangements are available that will accommodate a married nanny and spouse.

The employer provides normal meals and snacks for the live-out nanny while on duty. Full board is usually provided for the live-in nanny. Kitchen privileges during off-duty hours should be discussed with the employer. If a nanny requires or requests any special food, it is customary for employers to limit this to a specified dollar amount.

Paid Travel: Expenses for the nanny who provides child care while traveling are paid by the employer. Salary is paid as usual.

Car Insurance and Costs: If the nanny's car is used for work-related duties, the employer usually pays the difference between the normal insurance and the insurance required for a business use of the car. Mileage reimbursement and toll payments are also customary.

Benefits: Benefits may include health insurance, a car for personal as well as work use, paid vacation and holidays, and paid sick days. College tuition assistance, time off and financial assistance to attend a professional conference, or a clothing allowance for duty clothes or a uniform may be offered. Other perquisites available in some positions include opportunities for national or international travel or to live abroad with the employing family, membership in a country or sports club, or off-duty use of the employer's swimming pool, tennis court, or other amenities. It is not uncommon for the nanny to have to work a specified period of time before some benefits and privileges become effective.

Part-Time Employment: Salary for part-time nannies is usually based on an hourly rate. Benefits are prorated according to the number of hours per week the nanny works. For example, a nanny who works about half the hours a full-time nanny works may get five day's paid vacation instead of ten and three paid holidays instead of six. The employer may pay a part of the part-time nanny's health insurance cost.

Note: Conditions of work for foreign caregivers who come to the United States for one year under one of the government-approved au pair programs are determined by the regulations for these programs.

TAXES AND INSURANCE

A nanny should be aware of employer and employee responsibilities with respect to taxes and insurance. Failure to report wages and pay taxes is not only illegal and unethical, but it leaves the nanny without the employee protection and benefits provided by law. A nanny should never agree to be paid "under the table," that is, not report wages and pay taxes.

It is the employer's responsibility to obtain the necessary forms for reporting wages and paying taxes. The Internal Revenue Service (IRS) puts out a free publication, No. 196, entitled "Household Employers Tax Guide." This booklet, available at local IRS offices, provides helpful information about employer's federal responsibilities when a nanny is hired.

The employer is required to pay half the nanny's social security and Medicare taxes. The employer must also withhold the nanny's share of the tax from the nanny's paycheck and see that the entire tax is paid. Employers may choose to pay the entire tax themselves.

The employer is responsible for paying federal and state unemployment taxes. The employer must also carry workers' compensation insurance that covers an employee who sustains an injury on the job.

The nanny is responsible for federal, state, and any applicable local income taxes. These taxes are withheld from the nanny's paycheck by the employer who then pays them to the appropriate government agency. The employer must provide the nanny with a wage and tax statement in a copy of the IRS-W2 form before January 31 each year.

The nanny's employer is usually a private family. Sometimes, though, a nanny is employed by an agency that sends its nannies on assignment to families. In this situation, the agency must meet employer responsibilities for taxes and workers' compensation insurance.

Tax questions may be directed to the local IRS office, or by calling 1-800-829-1040. An accountant or tax specialist may also be consulted for current information on taxes.

LENGTH OF COMMITMENT

Continuity of care is important for children's well-being. In a long-term position, a nanny usually agrees to remain with the employing family for one year. In practice, many nannies remain in the same position far longer. However, a year is considered to be an appropriate commitment to make at the start of a job. It is better to keep or exceed a one-year commitment than to commit to two years and leave after 18 months.

Once made, the commitment should be kept. If the employer is fulfilling the provisions of the written employment agreement, the nanny must do the same. Breaking the commitment is unprofessional, disruptive to the children, and may earn the nanny a reputation for jumping from one job to another.

It bears repeating that a nanny should never begin work without a written employment agreement. The written agreement is essential if a nanny feels there are grounds for leaving before one year has been completed and wants to depart in a professional manner. If, for example, the nanny is expected to perform an increasing number of duties not included in the job description, the written agreement is necessary for trying to resolve the problem to the nanny's and the employer's satisfaction. If the problem cannot be resolved, the nanny has the written agreement to support the reason for leaving early. Although every reasonable effort should be made to remedy a problem, no one benefits from the nanny remaining in an unhappy situation.

Sometimes circumstances beyond the nanny's control make it necessary to break the commitment. Leaving because of serious personal illness or because the illness of someone in your family requires your extended involvement would be understandable.

Whatever the reason for resigning from a position, the nanny should give employers written notice. This is usually four weeks (or as specified in the written agreement), unless an emergency situation makes an earlier departure necessary. Leaving a position is discussed further in Chapter Ten.

CONTENTS OF THE WRITTEN EMPLOYMENT AGREEMENT

The employment arrangement is the business side of the nanny's job. It provides a framework for the nanny's work. As the employer, the family also has responsibilities. A nanny should be aware of what areas are typically covered in an employment agreement prior to discussing work arrangements with prospective employers.

There should be a written agreement, also referred to as a **contract**, before work begins. The nanny should be given a copy. The agreement can be tailored to fit the particular employment situation and changed at any time by mutual consent.

A trial period is included in the written agreement to allow either the nanny or employer to terminate the arrangement at an early stage without breaking a commitment. At the end of the trial period, both parties confirm the agreement if it is their intention to continue at least one year of employment.

A sample agreement appears in Appendix A. Suggested guidelines for any agreement include the following areas:

- ◆ A comprehensive nanny job description.
- ◆ Work commitment, including when employment begins, trial period, hours and days of work, overtime and how it

---

contract—A formal, written agreement between two or more people to do certain things.

is to be arranged, 24-hour duty, vacation, holidays, and sick days.

◆ Salary, including when and how it is to be paid and overtime compensation; tax withholding, social security and Medicare, unemployment taxes, and workers' compensation insurance.

◆ The nanny's live-in arrangements, if applicable, including the nanny's quarters, the nanny's access to other parts of the employer's home and use of amenities; house rules with regard to kitchen privileges, smoking, drinking, telephone use, and guests; mutual respect of private areas and private property.

◆ Transportation while on the job, including car insurance, repairs, and expenses.

◆ Expenses when the nanny travels with the family; expenses for children's activities and outings.

◆ Commitment to regular communications between the nanny and employer.

◆ Schedule and method for periodic evaluation of the nanny's work and salary review.

◆ Termination of agreement, including length of notice to be given and severance pay. Summary dismissal may be specified for serious misconduct.

JOB APPLICATION REQUIREMENTS

Whether you seek a nanny position through a placement agency or by dealing directly with prospective employers, you can expect that there will be certain job application requirements. In preparation for meeting these requirements, you will need to gather all relevant information, such as social security number, letters of recommendation, and documentation of education and training. You may be asked to complete an application form by an agency or a family. This must be done accurately, completely, and neatly. You should have the names, addresses, and telephone numbers of previous employers available, together with dates of employment. The same information should be available with regard to educational institutions attended.

Job application requirements vary from one situation to another, but the guidelines that follow will help you know what to expect and how to plan for your job applications.

Basic Application Requirements

Almost all application requirements stipulate a minimum age (18 years or older), education and experience relative to child care, work history, and verifiable references or letters of recommendation attesting to the candidate's good character and success in working with children. Usually three references or letters of recommendation are required.

You may also be asked if you are a smoker or non-smoker, a licensed driver, or a swimmer. Current certification in CPR (cardiopulmonary resuscitation) and first aid is often of interest and sometimes lifesaving certification. An agency may gather extensive information to help match nanny candidates with prospective employers.

Additional Requirements

You may be asked to consent to a medical examination, driving record check, criminal record check, credit history check, drug testing, or psychological testing. These may be done at the prospective employer's or agency's expense, but you should find out in advance if you have any responsibility for screening costs.

Employment Eligibility Verification

Employers are legally responsible for verifying that all new employees are eligible to work in the United States. You will be asked to produce proof of U.S. citizenship or evidence that you are an alien who is authorized to work. The employer and employee participate in completing Form I-9. The United States Immigration and Naturalization Service (INS) puts out a *Handbook for Employers* that explains the responsibilities of both employers and employees in the hiring verification process, including the documents needed and the form to be used. Questions should be directed to the local INS office.

Licensing

Although a license to work as a nanny is not usually required, it should be determined if there are any state or local regulations applicable in the place you intend to seek employment.

BIBLIOGRAPHY

Child Care Action Campaign. *Finding and Hiring a Qualified In-Home Caregiver*, CCAC Information Guide 20. New York: Child Care Action Campaign.

Davis, D. (1991). *The Nanny Match Book*. Austin, TX: Laurel House Press.

Davis, L.E. (1988). "Job Descriptions for Nursery Nurses Working in Private Homes." *National Nanny Newsletter* 4(2), 17.

International Nanny Association. "Conference '95 T-Shirt Survey—Part II: Nanny Response." *INAVision* Summer 1996, 6.

"Nanny News Survey of Nanny Experience." *Nanny News*, March/April 1996, 1, 6–8.

Pelletier, E.S. (1994). *How to Hire a Nanny*. Englewood, CO: Andre and Lanier.

Raffin, P.M. (1996). *The Good Nanny Book*. New York: Berkley Books.

"Recommended Practices for Nanny Placement Agencies," *INA 1995 Directory*, 27–29. Norfolk, NE: International Nanny Association.

Thomas, C.H. (1995). *The Complete Nanny Guide*. New York: Avon Books.

U.S. Department of Labor (1994). *Handy Reference Guide to the Fair Labor Standards Act*, revised October 1994, WH Publication 1282. Washington, DC: U.S. Government Printing Office.

U.S. Department of Labor (1979). *Regulations, Part 552: Application of the Fair Labor Standards Act to Domestic Service*, revised August, 1979, WH Publication 1409. Washington, DC: U.S. Government Printing Office.

U.S. Department of Labor (1996). "Fair Labor Standards Act Amendments of 1996," ESA Fact Sheet No. 96-13. Washington, DC: U.S. Department of Labor.

U.S. Department of the Treasury, International Revenue Service (1995). *Household Employer's Tax Guide*, Pub. 926. Washington, DC: U.S. Government Printing Office.

U.S. Immigration and Naturalization Service (1991). *Handbook for Employers: Instructions for Completing Form I-9*. Washington, DC: U.S. Government Printing Office.

Chapter 8

Interviewing

TOPICS

- ◆ Introduction
- ◆ Developing a Philosophy of Child Care
- ◆ Portfolio Preparation
- ◆ Résumé Preparation
- ◆ Preparing for an Interview
- ◆ Issues to Discuss
- ◆ Conclusion and Follow Up
- ◆ Accepting a Position

Terms to Know

philosophy   *perquisite*
principle

INTRODUCTION

The interview plays a significant role in helping you obtain the nanny position you want. Careful planning enables you to present yourself positively as a candidate for the jobs that interest you. You will be judged by prospective employers on the basis of skills, personality, adaptability, and how well you respond to questions. Careful planning before an interview also enables you to gather the information about the family and the nanny position that you will need to make a job decision.

DEVELOPING A PHILOSOPHY OF CHILD CARE

A **philosophy** of child care is the expression of what you think is most important in caring for children. It reflects the **principles** that guide your interactions with children. In order to discuss your principles of care with parents, it is necessary to clarify them in your own mind and to sum them up in a simple statement or philosophy of child care. Put in writing, your philosophy becomes part of your professional portfolio (see pages 161–163).

Give careful thought about how you will articulate your deeply held principles of care. The written summary should be general enough to apply to all young children from birth on. It should be positive. State what you believe good child care is rather than what it is not. Make it *yours*. Early childhood professionals share some fundamental principles of practice (see Chapter Three), but each individual has a unique contribution to make in promoting children's well-being. You may want to reexamine your philosophy from time to time and alter it to take into account your new experiences and perspectives.

philosophy—A particular set of principles for guiding conduct.

principle—A rule of right conduct.

As you go through the process of defining your own philosophy, identify some of the elements of good caregiving such as: treating children with respect, recognizing each child as an individual, providing responsive care, building trust and security, recognizing the value of daily care routines in nurturing all aspects of development, allowing children to try to solve their own problems, and modeling behavior you want to teach children. There may be other elements that are important to you. Make a list of your priorities before creating your own personal statement.

Crystallize your philosophy in a few clear sentences and type them neatly on one side of a sheet of paper. Make sure that spelling, grammar, and punctuation are correct. Use gender-neutral language. Two examples of a philosophy of child care follow:

> I believe child care should be approached with patience, a sense of humor, and confidence in the child's own ability to learn and succeed. The adult's role is to provide a safe and nurturing environment in which each child has maximum opportunity to develop physically, intellectually, socially, and emotionally. I think it is important to recognize the individuality of each child and provide care that responds to the individual child. Reasonable limits, consistently maintained, are necessary to give children a sense of security and help them gain self-control. As a nanny, I know it is also important to model the behavior I want to teach.

> I believe a happy, secure childhood is every child's birthright. From infancy, children need to know they are valued. Trust and confidence develop when adults respond to children's physical needs, play and talk with them, and encourage them to explore and discover within safe limits. Discipline should be appropriate to the age of the child and stated in positive terms, with the goal of helping the child gain self-control. It is important to me to respect each child and respond to individual needs, interests, and abilities.

PORTFOLIO PREPARATION

A portfolio is a collection of documents and other materials put together in an organized way to represent your professional qualifications. Arranged in a folder, these materials can easily be presented for prospective employers to review during a job interview.

Select a plain, professional-looking folder, either a pocket folder or a three-ring binder. Identify it with a typed label, for example:

> **LYNN L. JONES**
> Professional Nanny

All items to be included must be neat and clean. If a ring binder is used, holes must be punched evenly and hole reinforcements used when necessary. Protective plastic covers may be used. The original of a document that would be difficult or impossible to replace should not be used—for example, any certificate, award or diploma, and letters of recommendation. Make copies of such documents for your portfolio and keep originals in a separate file in a safe place. If there is a possibility you will want to leave some information from your portfolio with prospective employers, have extra copies ready. You do not want to dismantle your portfolio, but you may want to leave copies of letters of recommendation or a list of persons who have agreed to provide you with references. You will certainly want to have copies of your résumé available (see pages 163–165).

Information to be shared with prospective employers should be accurate and complete. A negative impression of the candidate is created when a reference's telephone number is missing or incorrect, or a name or address is incomplete or misspelled.

It is both wise and courteous to ask people if they are willing to serve as references for you before listing them. References should be persons who can attest to your character and your professional competence in working with children. Relatives and close family friends should not be asked to be references or write letters of recommendation.

Additions can be made to a portfolio as new experiences and achievements are acquired. The following basic items are suggested:

- ◆ Your typed or word processed philosophy of child care.
- ◆ Your typed or word processed résumé.

- Three verifiable letters of recommendation or a typed or word processed list of references, with complete names, telephone numbers, and addresses.
- Nanny training certificate, if applicable.
- College transcripts, if applicable.
- First aid and CPR certificates.
- Any other certificates relative to child care (for example, high school child-care training program, lifesaving).
- Any awards relative to child care.
- Any other written evidence of the nanny competencies you possess.
- Samples of children's activities.

Other items to consider for inclusion:

- Samples of record-keeping forms to be used in employment.
- Description sheet of your nanny training program if applicable.
- A favorite poem or prose passage that reflects your approach to the care of children (typed or word processed).

RÉSUMÉ PREPARATION

A résumé is a concise summary of your education, employment experience, related data, and employment objective. You should have a copy of your résumé available for each job interview. If you are seeking a position through a nanny placement agency, your résumé can become part of your file there. If you respond to a nanny job opening by mail, your résumé and a cover letter (see pages 165–167) introduce you and your qualifications to prospective employers.

There are several ways to present your qualifications in a résumé. It is a personal document and there are no set rules governing how it should be done. There are, however, some worthwhile points to remember. The finished product should look as if it were the result of careful thought and execution. A résumé must be organized so that the reader can easily see the qualifications that make you a good candidate for the job. It should be short and to the point. It is only one of the tools used in the process of seeking employment. There are other opportunities to provide information in telephone conversations, personal interviews, and cover letters. A résumé should be pleasing to the eye. Use the best quality typing and paper available to you. Consider using a word processor. It not only helps to create a professional-looking résumé, but has the added advantage of keeping the information stored and available for easy updating when necessary. A résumé should not look cramped. Plenty of white space—that is, margins and space between sections—add to a résumé's attractiveness. Résumés are usually written in an objective style that eliminates the use of "I" and saves space. Arrange experiences in reverse chronological order, that is, put the most recent first. A résumé must be proofread very carefully to ensure that it makes sense and contains no errors. Abbreviations should not be used.

In planning a résumé, gather all relevant data, including dates, on a worksheet. Create headings for education, career-related experience, additional experience, additional skills, honors/awards if applicable, and activities/interests. Write down everything you have done and achieved under the headings. Do not overlook skills and experience that can transfer from one job to another, particularly if you are at an early stage of your career. For example, work as a cashier prior to nanny training may appear to have little relationship to child care, but it suggests trustworthiness and basic job skills such as punctuality and dependability. Work as a waiter or waitress to pay for college suggests not only good interpersonal skills and stamina, but independence, ability to manage time, and a high value placed on education. Hobbies and interests can translate into skills of interest to nanny employers. For example, musical or artistic talent, proficiency in a foreign language, interest in camping and outdoor activities, or the ability to ski, skate, or swim can be an asset in some nanny situations. (NOTE: Swimming should be referred to as an interest or hobby rather than a skill unless you have current lifesaving certification.) Include memberships in professional early childhood organizations. Volunteer work, summer jobs, internships, or foreign travel can also support a nanny's qualifications.

Although you probably will not include all the worksheet information in your résumé, reviewing everything you have accomplished is useful preparation for the interview when there will be more opportunity to let prospective employers know who you are and what you can do. Qualifications for a job must always be presented truthfully and without exaggeration, but underestimating what you have to offer should also be avoided.

Personal information (age, date of birth, marital status, number of children) is not necessary. If it is appropriate to the position, personal data may be included in a cover letter or disclosed at the interview. References do not belong in a résumé. The final line usually reads "References upon request," although this may be omitted if the space could be better used elsewhere. A prospective employer will require references at some point in the interviewing process anyway.

Cover Letters

If you are responding to an opening for a nanny position by mail, a cover letter should accompany your résumé. The letter tells prospective employers why they should read your résumé and consider you as a candidate.

The letter begins with a statement about why you are writing. If you are responding to an advertisement, refer to it in the opening paragraph. In the body of the letter, introduce yourself, explain why you are interested in the position, and how your qualifications make you suited to it. In the conclusion, express your willingness to provide more information and include a means of reaching you to arrange an interview. Type or word process your letter on a good grade of letter-sized bond paper and use a matching envelope. *Make sure spelling, punctuation, and grammar are correct.* Make a copy of this letter and any other work-related correspondence for your own files.

A sample résumé and cover letter appear in Figures 8.1 and 8.2.

LESLIE M. GOODE

10 Erie Close, Cleveland, Ohio 44100

(216) 555-9170

OBJECTIVE

To use my child-care education and experience in a home-based position.

EDUCATION

Nannies of Cleveland School, Lakewood, Ohio. Nanny Training Diploma (May, 1997).

Riveredge High School, Avon, Ohio. High School Diploma and Child-Care Program Certificate, 1995. Outstanding Student award.

EXPERIENCE

Field Placement: Bethany Child-Care Center, North Montessori School, private home. Observed and cared for infants through preschoolers in a variety of supervised settings during nanny training.

Teacher Assistant: ABC Child Care, Elyria, Ohio, 1995–96. Assisted with planning and providing daily care and play activities for toddlers. Substituted in infant room.

Summer Program Assistant: Avon Board of Education, 1993 and 1995. Planned and provided a range of activities for children five to seven years in an all-day program.

Child Care: For several families on a regular basis. Responsible for all aspects of care during parents' absence. Children two months to nine years, including infant twins, 1992–1997.

ADDITIONAL EXPERIENCE

Summer Exchange Student, England, 1994.

Volunteer: St. John's Hospital, 1993–96.

ADDITIONAL SKILLS

Cardiopulmonary Resuscitation (infant/child and adult) and First Aid certificates, 1997. Ice skating, piano playing.

ACTIVITIES/INTERESTS

Member: National Association for the Education of Young Children, International Nanny Association, National Association of Nannies. Travel, swimming, reading.

Figure 8.1   Sample résumé.

April 20, 1997

Mr. and Mrs. Eric Peters
2233 Jefferson Drive
Alexandria, VA 22444

Dear Mr. and Mrs. Peters,

I am responding to your advertisement for a live-in nanny in today's *New York Times*. I am currently completing a nanny training program and will graduate on May 17. I am 20 years old, single, and have no restrictions on relocation and travel.

The enclosed résumé outlines my child-care education and experience, which I believe have prepared me for the high level of care you are seeking for your three children. Since you indicate that one of your children is a newborn, my experience with infants may be of particular interest to you.

If you would like additional information after you have reviewed my qualifications, please contact me at the number below after 6 P.M. Following an initial telephone interview, I could be available for a personal interview during a weekend.

I look forward to hearing from you. Thank you for your consideration.

Sincerely yours,

Leslie M. Goode

Leslie M. Goode
10 Erie Close
Cleveland, OH 44100
(216) 555-9170

Enclosure

Figure 8.2 Sample cover letter.

PREPARING FOR AN INTERVIEW

Careful preparation for an actual interview helps you to approach it with confidence and make it a positive experience in the search for the nanny position that is right for you.

Interview Arrangements

Initially, you and prospective employers should talk on the telephone and obtain enough information from each other to determine if the next step is a personal interview. It is especially important to have a thorough telephone interview when a personal interview would involve traveling some distance (interviewing for an out-of-town or out-of-state job is discussed more fully on pages 174 and 175).

Assuming that the position for which you are having a personal interview is within reasonable driving distance, confirm that you have the family's correct name and address. Obtain directions and write them down to take with you, together with a map. Determine how long it will take you to get to the interview. Good planning allows extra time for possible traffic delays and for finding the house. *Arriving late for an interview creates a bad impression and may disqualify you altogether from having an interview.* Avoid arriving early. This can be inconvenient or annoying to prospective employers. In the event an emergency compels you to cancel an interview or be late, telephone prospective employers promptly and apologize. Carry their telephone number with you when you set out for the interview, together with change for a telephone call.

When you are going to interview outside your own hometown, obtain information about the community before the interview. This provides you with background for asking relevant questions about the community at the interview and for responding to prospective employers if they ask why you want to relocate there.

What to Take

In addition to your portfolio (see pages 161–163), there are several other items you should take with you for an interview. Keep them in a folder separate from your portfolio folder so they are organized and easy to reach. The following items are suggested:

◆ Paper, writing instrument.

◆ List of questions you want to be sure to ask.

◆ Health insurance information. If employers offer health insurance benefits, they will want to know the plan you have or intend to obtain. Investigate before you start interviewing if you need coverage. Health insurance through a professional organization is one possibility to consider (see Appendix D).

◆ Guidelines for a nanny job description/employment agreement.

◆ Extra copies of your résumé, letters of recommendation and/or list of persons who have agreed to be your references (with addresses and telephone numbers), and your philosophy of child care to leave with prospective employers.

In addition, you may want to take your special play bag of basic creative materials and simple stories to use with the children and put them at ease with you.

Personal Appearance

Appropriate attire and immaculate grooming are essential for looking and feeling your professional best at an interview. While it is usually wise to err on the side of dressing conservatively, formal business attire is not suitable for a nanny interview. You want to look and feel comfortable, so you are just as much at ease holding the baby or sitting on the carpet with the toddler as you are presenting yourself professionally to parents. For women, a simple, classic dress with a coordinating blazer and low-heeled shoes would make a good impression. An alternative would be a nice skirt and simple blouse with the blazer. The blazer can be removed when you are interacting with children or if it is warm. For men, good, washable slacks, dress shirt and tie or a nice sport shirt, together with a navy blazer would be suitable. You may still feel overdressed if the family greets you in shorts, jeans, or even swimsuits (this has been known to happen), but casual dress is inappropriate for the candidate.

Regardless of what you decide to wear, grooming is as important as attire in creating an impression of professionalism. Clothing must be cleaned and pressed, shoes polished, nails spotless, and hair clean and neatly arranged. Check for runs or wrinkles in hose, worn heels on shoes, and similar details of grooming before an interview. Fragrance, makeup, and jewelry should be discreet (see pages 117–123 for dress and grooming for nannies).

At the Interview

When you arrive for the interview, greet prospective employers by name and introduce yourself. Allow them to initiate a handshake and let yours be warm and firm. Do not call prospective employers by their first names until you are invited to do so. Wait for them to ask you to be seated. Avoid comments about the home. Keep in mind constantly that this is an employment interview and not a social call, even though the setting is a home.

During the interview, use good posture. Avoid looking too tense or too casual. Be aware that interview nervousness can make you appear aloof or even hostile. This is an opportunity to allow your personality and unique professional style to show. Maintain good eye contact but avoid outstaring.

Listen to questions carefully and assume they are all asked with a purpose that is related to the job. Avoid talking too much. Questions should be answered candidly and completely, but the urge to expand or repeat, often the result of nervousness, should be controlled. Poor grammar and slang expressions mark a candidate as unprofessional. For example, refer to children as children, not kids. Humor should be used cautiously and in good taste during an interview. Above all, focus on your professional experience and not your personal life. Highlight your qualifications without exaggerating them or appearing conceited.

Show a sincere interest in the children and the family as a whole. Ask if you may hold the baby. If the children are not in evidence, inquire as to when you can meet them. Let prospective employers see that you possess essential nanny qualities of courtesy, tact, and enthusiasm. Never speak of previous employers in a disparaging way.

Be prepared to answer some commonly asked questions, such as:

- ◆ Why did you choose to become a nanny?
- ◆ What have you learned from other jobs you have held?
- ◆ How did your previous employers treat you?
- ◆ Why did you leave your last job?
- ◆ Why should we hire you as our nanny?
- ◆ What are your strengths?
- ◆ What is your major weakness?
- ◆ What are your long-range plans?
- ◆ What is most important to you in raising children?
- ◆ Tell us about yourself.

ISSUES TO DISCUSS

It is the responsibility of employers to prepare a nanny job description prior to interviewing, but this is not always done (see pages 146–149). A nanny should come to interviews prepared to ask questions about duties and other aspects of the job that will become the substance of the written employment agreement. Some questions will depend on the particular nanny situation, while others need to be addressed for any nanny job. Additional questions will come to mind during the interview.

You will demonstrate your professionalism and enthusiasm for being a nanny by focusing questions on the children and parents' childrearing practices. This will also provide you with necessary information for determining if this is a situation in which you can work successfully. Reasonable agreement on how to care for young children is essential for a good working relationship between the nanny and employers and for consistency of child care.

Express your philosophy of child care and ask parents about theirs. Since parents have ultimate authority over how their children are raised, you will have to decide how flexible you are willing to be in order to work with any given family. It is important to discuss the parents' method of discipline. If physical punishment is an issue, you need to make it clear that under no circumstances would you use it. Be prepared to explain alternative ways of guiding children's behavior that you have found effective.

When you ask questions about the children, you tell parents a lot about your knowledge of child development and appropriate care. At the same time, you learn what parents expect from their nanny. Depending on the situation, other issues to discuss include the children's daily routines, health and safety concerns, television watching policy, children's favorite activities and toys, infant feeding, family food preferences, sibling relationships, toilet training, separation anxiety, nursery school, and the child's previous experiences with caregivers.

You need to find out about your responsibilities. For example, will they include shopping for the children and planning and preparing their meals? Will you be expected to take children to doctor and dentist appointments, arrange outings to parks, the zoo, beach, or other places, or provide swimming supervision (remember that this should not be undertaken without a parent or lifeguard present unless you have a valid lifesaving certificate)? Determine who is responsible for cleaning the nanny's and the children's quarters, including routine care and heavy or seasonal cleaning. It is advisable to inquire if other household staff is employed. If there is not a housekeeper or a regular cleaning service, the nanny may be expected to assume household duties beyond those related to child care. Find out whose responsibility it is to supervise other staff or train a substitute caregiver. If there are pets, ask if you have any responsibility for their care and supervision.

Information about how you will fit into the household is important, especially in a live-in situation. When parents are at home, do the nanny, children and parents eat together and, if so, what is the nanny's responsibility for meal preparation and clean-up? What areas of the house are available to you when you are off duty, or are you expected to go to your own quarters? What accommodations are provided and are you allowed to decorate your room as you wish (the nanny should be shown the accommodations at an appropriate point in the interview). Other issues may include policy on guests, alcohol consumption when off duty, curfews, and whether the nanny is required to wear a uniform.

Salary, benefits, and additional **perquisites** are important considerations in any job search, but a candidate should not give the impression that they are a primary concern. Wait until employers raise the issue of compensation and related matters or until you are confident enough of their interest in you to ask.

Although you may have requirements of your own, try to keep your mind open to alternatives as you listen to what is proposed. There may be room for negotiation in the overall compensation package.

You should verify that the employer assumes responsibility for tax withholding, social security tax, unemployment taxes, and carrying workers' compensation insurance at an appropriate point in the interview process and before accepting a job offer.

You will want to know if employers intend to put the terms of employment in a written agreement. You should also ask if you may speak with the previous nanny and/or another reference for the family.

Many of these issues will arise naturally during the interview, especially if parents have given careful thought to employing a nanny. Nevertheless, without giving the impression that you are interrogating prospective employers, make sure that you leave the interview with the information needed for a job decision. Sometimes a nanny who is a strong candidate for the job is invited for a second interview. This gives both the nanny and prospective employers another opportunity to determine if this is likely to be a successful arrangement. The second interview is

---

perquisite—An extra benefit or privilege accompanying a job. Sometimes referred to colloquially as a perk.

typically less formal than the first and the nanny spends more time with the children.

While interviewing, do not overlook observation as a way to learn more about the family and its lifestyle. Is the house formal or informal? Is it extremely tidy, extremely messy or reasonably neat, clean and "lived-in"? Are the children included in the interview and are their playthings in evidence? Parents may want to conduct the interview without interruption for a while, but eventually a nanny needs to meet the children and be able to observe parent/child interactions. Look for clues to family pastimes and fun; for example, Are there books in evidence? Is the television in use? What kinds of toys do the children have and is there sports equipment to be seen?

Interviewing usually takes place at the prospective employers' home, but sometimes the first meeting is held at the placement agency office, a restaurant, or some other common ground. Eventually the nanny needs to see the family in the home setting and meet the children before making a job decision.

Out-of-Town Interviewing

The information you need to obtain about an out-of-town or out-of-state position is basically the same as it is for a position that is fairly close to you. However, the first in-depth interview is conducted by telephone. Since this will be a long-distance call lasting an hour or more, it is customary for the employers to pay for it.

It is important for the nanny and the employers to take a telephone interview just as seriously as a personal one. Conduct yourself as you would in person. Be ready with a list of the information you want to obtain and a writing instrument and paper for notes. Use a telephone in a quiet room and ask your family or roommates not to disturb you (try to arrange the interview at a time when a lengthy call will not inconvenience others).

The next step in the out-of-town or out-of-state interview process is a personal interview, with the employer paying the nanny's travel expenses by plane or car. This step should not be taken until you are almost certain that you would accept the position if it was offered to you, contingent on a positive visit with the family in their own surroundings. It is unfair and unnecessary for a nanny to waste the employer's time and money when factors that would make a job unacceptable can be discovered in a thorough telephone interview. On the other hand, no nanny should accept a position without a personal interview and the opportunity to see parents and children in their own home.

When you travel some distance for a personal interview, you will usually be invited to stay overnight. Keep in mind that from your arrival to your departure, the whole visit is the interview. When you and employers sit down for a long talk about your qualifications, the job and work arrangements, it may be after the children are in bed and when you are all wearing the casual slacks or shorts you wore to play with the children and have a cookout. Alternatively, perhaps arrangements have been made for evening child care so you and employers can talk while having dinner at a nice restaurant. The format may not be the same as a local interview, but you and the employers will be learning about each other and forming impressions throughout the visit.

Take all the items that you would take to a personal interview closer to home (see pages 168 and 169). Pack as lightly as you can, choosing clothes that are versatile and coordinate well together. A nanny arriving with a large suitcase for a weekend will not create a good impression.

Inasmuch as there will be no opportunity for a second personal interview in this situation, the visit must be used to full advantage. If a job offer is made and accepted, details of the work arrangement should be established while you are there. Relocation plans and expenses should be discussed. Be sure to write down all the information you will need later for starting the job.

CONCLUSION AND FOLLOW UP

The employer usually indicates that an interview is at an end by standing up and thanking the candidate for coming. You should rise when the employer does. Assuming you are very interested in the job, this is your opportunity to sum up why you think you would be a suitable nanny for this family and ask for another opportunity to talk together. Express your thanks for the interview upon leaving.

Immediately after an interview, organize the information you have obtained about the position and family, so that you can compare it with information about other job possibilities you are exploring. Write the information down and keep it safe and private in a folder. Confidentiality is important during the interviewing process because you are already acquiring personal information about families.

Always follow up after an interview. Within a day of the interview write a brief note of thanks and reiterate your interest in the position (see Figure 8.3 for a sample follow-up note). If you have not heard from the employers by the time they indicated a decision would be made, call them. These steps demonstrate your interest, enthusiasm, and professionalism.

Use each interview as a learning experience. Interviewing is a skill that, like other skills, can be improved. Evaluate what you said, what you might have said, and what might have been better left unsaid. Evaluate how the employer responded to what you said, how well you listened, and whether you learned what you needed to know about the job. Ask yourself:

- Did I present my professional qualifications effectively?
- What points did I make that seemed to interest the employer in particular?
- Did I take all the materials I needed for the interview?
- Did I feel comfortable and appropriate in the clothes I chose to wear?
- Did I maintain good posture and eye contact?
- Did I keep nervousness under control?
- Did I recognize and use opportunities to highlight my qualifications?
- Did I answer questions completely and candidly without talking too much?

45 Daisy Lane
Greenville, OH 45678
January 22, 1997

Mr. and Mrs. Peter Grace
1234 Echo Court
Upper Arlington, OH 43210

Dear Mr. and Mrs. Grace,

I enjoyed meeting with you and *your children yesterday. I appreciated the time you spent with me.

If you have further questions, please do not hesitate to contact me. I hope I may have the opportunity to talk with you further about the nanny position and look forward to hearing from you.

Sincerely,

Chris Gordon

Chris Gordon
(614) 555-8765

Note: You may wish to put name(s) of child(ren) here.

Figure 8.3   Sample follow-up letter after an interview.

- ◆ Did I ask questions about the children?
- ◆ Did I find out about the aspects of the job that are important to me?
- ◆ Are there any improvements I should make for future interviews?

ACCEPTING A POSITION

When you receive a job offer, or perhaps more than one, the next task is to review the information you gathered and wrote down during the interview process. Note the advantages and disadvantages of each position, depending on what is important to you. This helps you to identify the job that best matches your requirements. Do not allow a placement agency, prospective employers, or anyone else to persuade you to accept a job you do not really want. Notify the employer as soon as you have decided to accept a position. It is courteous to inform other employers who have shown interest in you that you are no longer available and thank them. If you are working with an agency, follow its procedure for accepting a position.

Depending on the circumstances, another meeting between you and the employer may be necessary to finalize and sign the written employment agreement, a copy of which comes to you. Arrangements for the start of employment may still need to be made (see Chapter Nine for starting employment). If you are currently engaged in any kind of employment, proper notice must be given to your employer.

BIBLIOGRAPHY

Davis, D. (1987). "Contract Issues." *Nanny Handbook*. Claremont, CA: International Nanny Association.

Davis, L.E. (1987). "Selecting a Job as a Nursery Nurse in a Private Family" (paper). Hungerford, UK: Norland Nursery Training College.

Forney, D. (1988). "Conducting an In-Depth Interview with a Family." *National Nanny Newsletter* 4(2), 8.

Ohio Bureau of Employment Services (1986). *How to Get a Job*. Columbus, OH: OBES.

Raffin, P.M. (1996). *The Good Nanny Book*. New York: Berkley Books.

Rice, R. (1987). *The American Nanny*. New York: Harper and Row.

"Tips on Participating in an Employment Interview." *Journal of Employment Counseling*, 21(4), December 1984.

Chapter 9

When Employment Begins

TOPICS

- ◆ Introduction
- ◆ Relocation
- ◆ Orientation
- ◆ Managing Your Time
- ◆ Trial Period

Terms to Know

probation

INTRODUCTION

Starting a new job brings a mix of excitement and apprehension. Being organized and informed makes the transition easier and minimizes possible problems.

The nanny who has accepted a position in a well-informed way has a good base from which to begin actual employment. This includes having had at least one in-person interview with prospective employers, visits to the home, and opportunities to spend time with the children and observe the parents interacting with their children. It also includes having done some research on the new community if relocation is involved and having a written employment agreement before the first day of work. Nevertheless, there will still be a great deal to learn and do to get off to a good start.

RELOCATION

Whether your new job takes you 50 miles from where you are now living or across the country, there are many practical matters that require attention and, depending on your particular situation, include the following:

- ◆ Notify the Post Office of your move on a change of address order form. The United States Postal Service offers a free booklet, "Mover's Guide" (Publication 75), which contains the necessary form (PS Form 3575) and tips for making moving easier. The booklet is available at post offices. In order to avoid delay in receiving mail at the new address, the change of address form should be submitted at least 30 days before the move.

- ◆ The post office also provides postcards (PS Form 3675) for notifying family, friends, businesses, banks, insurance companies, credit card companies, doctors, dentists, state and federal tax authorities, and other government agencies of a change of address.

◆ Notify magazines of the change of address as early as possible. It can take six to eight weeks for the change to become effective. A toll-free number or address for making the change is usually listed at the beginning of the publication.

◆ Make your travel arrangements, coordinating them with your employer. Usually the employer pays for the nanny's transportation to a new job. Confirm the time and date of your arrival with your employer about a week before moving. Carry the employer's address and telephone number in a handy place and any directions you will need.

◆ If you are taking your car, make sure it is in roadworthy condition. If you are moving to a major city, you may determine that it is easier to use public transportation than have the responsibility of a car.

◆ If you are moving to another state, you will need a new driver's license and license plates for your car. Obtain information from the Auto and Driver's License Bureau (State Department of Motor Vehicles) closest to your employer.

◆ Transfer membership in AAA (American Automobile Association).

◆ Notify national associations to which you belong of your change of address. If they have state or local chapters, transfer your membership.

◆ Arrange to close or transfer your bank account.

◆ Register to vote in your new community. Contact the local board of elections for registration information.

◆ Obtain a library card at your new public library.

◆ Make sure you are in good health. Have any necessary medical, dental and eye examinations done before moving. Ask your current health professionals about finding new providers.

◆ NOTE: Whether you are relocating or not, notify your insurance agent if you will be using your car for work-related purposes such as running errands and transporting children. Additional insurance protection will probably be needed (see page 151).

ORIENTATION

The first week or two after a nanny arrives is a period of adjustment for the nanny, the parents, and the children. The following guidelines are designed to help you think ahead about what you will need to know to settle into the home and community and to meet your responsibilities to the children and your employers.

The Home

Orientation to the home should include a complete tour of the house and outside areas, demonstrations of equipment you will use, and instruction in safety and security measures and emergency procedures.

It is important for the nanny to have a thorough orientation to the new environment in order to provide safe, appropriate child care. It helps to clarify terms of employment related to the nanny's use of the employer's space and property. It makes the nanny feel comfortable, confident, and able to get on with the job. The following suggested guidelines could be used to develop a checklist with employers, adapted to the particular home and employment situation:

- ◆ Each parent's place of work and telephone numbers.
- ◆ Telephone number of the person(s) designated by the parents to be called in an emergency if parents cannot be reached, neighbors' names and telephone numbers as appropriate.
- ◆ Emergency telephone number(s) for contacting emergency medical, police, or fire services.
- ◆ Poison control center telephone number (this, together with the emergency numbers above should be posted at each telephone in the house; the address and directions to the house should also be by each telephone).
- ◆ The names, addresses, and telephone numbers of the preferred physician, dentist, and hospital.

◆ Location of first aid and home nursing supplies.

◆ The emergency plan in case of fire. The location of the fire extinguisher and how to operate it.

◆ The plan in case of a tornado, severe storm, earthquake, or similar emergency that may occur in the region where you are working.

◆ The home security alarm system.

◆ Instructions for locking the house and closing windows when you are taking the children out and no one is home or when you are responsible for locking up at night; the keys you will need. *NOTE:* Keys to your employer's home must always be kept safe in your possession.

◆ Safety features on the door (spy-hole, chain) to use when establishing a caller's identity.

◆ The safety precautions that the parents have in place to protect children from harm both indoors and outside (including safety measures for a swimming pool or any other body of water, however small). *NOTE:* Although a house may have been "child-proofed," no environment is completely free of dangers. It will be your responsibility to make your own safety assessment of the child's environment, provide supervision and be constantly alert to potential dangers.

◆ Instructions for operating all kitchen appliances; for example, stove, microwave, toaster oven, food processor, coffee maker, trash compactor, dishwasher.

◆ Location of cookware and implements; also the china, glasses, cutlery, and table linens for the nanny's and children's use.

◆ Storage of food staples, paper products, and other household supplies.

◆ Location of cleaning supplies and equipment; instructions for using the vacuum cleaner and changing the disposable bag, if there is one.

◆ Instructions for operating the clothes washer and dryer, instructions for any preferred laundry methods or schedule, location of iron and ironing board.

◆ The names and telephone numbers of appliance repair companies, plumber, electrician, and local gas and electricity companies.

◆ The schedule and procedure for the diaper service, if this is used.

◆ Instructions for any necessary separating of trash or recycling and where it should be put.

◆ Instructions for operating the television, VCR, computer, fax machine, or any other equipment you may be asked to use.

◆ The preferred temperature settings for the house in cold and hot weather. Location of the thermostats and any instructions with regard to setting the heat or air conditioning.

◆ Location of the fuse box and instructions for changing a fuse.

◆ Location of the shut-off for the main water supply.

◆ The name, telephone number, and address of the preferred car repair company.

◆ Instructions for operating the employer's car if the nanny is to use it; car insurance information.

◆ The parts of the house that are off limits to the nanny (as described in the employment agreement).

◆ The nanny's quarters in a live-in position (issues such as cleaning and maintenance of the nanny's quarters, putting pictures on the walls, and personalizing the room in other ways, and assuring the nanny's privacy are usually discussed at the time of hiring and described in the employment agreement; these should be reviewed when the nanny moves in).

◆ Instructions with respect to others who provide household services, such as a housekeeper or gardener.

◆ Instructions for the care of domestic pets for which the nanny may have some responsibility (as described in the employment agreement).

The Child

Your primary responsibility is to maintain a safe and healthy environment that nurtures the physical, emotional, intellectual, and social development of the children in your care. In order to do this successfully, you will need to obtain all pertinent background information about each child, usually from the parents. This information, together with your own observations, will form the basis for planning and providing appropriate care for the individual child.

The skilled nanny will respond with patience and sensitivity to the child during the period of adjustment to the new caregiver. The child may be coping with the loss of a previous nanny to whom there was deep attachment. On the other hand, it may be a new experience for the child to have both parents away at work all day and be left in the care of a nanny. Knowledge of the child's health, development, personality, habits, and environment is essential to helping the child accept the changed situation. Make notes as you discuss the child with parents and keep them in a safe, private place for reference. The following guidelines are suggested:

- Child's health and development history, including allergies, immunizations, and health screenings; physician recommendations at present; and any parental concerns about health and development.

- Typical daily routines and requirements (meals/infant feeding, rest and sleep, play, personal hygiene) and any information relevant to the routines (for example, food preferences, settling down to sleep, fears, self-help skills).

- Toilet training process and the words the child understands and uses.

- Favorite toys, activities, and outings.

- How the child gets along with other children and adults; any difficulty with separation.

- Parents' approach to discipline and setting limits; any parental concern about the child's behavior.

- Depending on the child's age, other issues to discuss with parents may include their approach to sex education, drug abuse awareness, and prevention of sexual abuse.

- Introduction of the nanny to the child's physician and dentist before the need for care arises.

- Written authorization for the nanny to seek medical care for the child in the event parents cannot be reached (health insurance information should be included).

- Written policy, established by the parents in consultation with the physician, for the nanny to administer medication to the child.

- Introduction of the nanny to the child's teachers and school; the school's name, address, and telephone number; the school schedule and any transportation in which the nanny will be involved.

- The child's friends; this information should include the names, addresses, and telephone numbers of any family with whom the child exchanges visits and the house rules for visits.

- Close relationships in the child's life, such as grandparents, and what the nanny's role will be when grandparents or others visit.

- When parents are divorced, information about child-custody arrangements and visits with the noncustodial parent, as appropriate to the nanny's role.

- Child's quarters including bedroom, playroom, and bathroom; where clothing, toys, and supplies are kept; cleaning routines for the child's quarters and equipment.

- Outdoor play area, equipment and toys; house rules for where tricycles, bicycles, and similar equipment may be ridden.

- Instructions for the correct use of child's equipment such as the car safety seat and how to collapse and put up the stroller or portable crib.

The Employer

The foundations of the nanny/employer relationship were laid at the time of hiring when the employment agreement was discussed and written. The development of a good working relationship begins in earnest as you assume your responsibilities and the agreement is implemented.

In addition to meeting your responsibilities to the children, your responsibilities to your employers include adapting to their home, complying with house rules, and adjusting to their way of doing things.

The thoughtful nanny recognizes that this is a period of adjustment for employers, too. Like the child, they may be sorry to see the previous nanny go, or perhaps their experience was not a positive one. In either event, past experience may influence the time it takes employers to accept and trust a new nanny. Alternatively, this may be the first time they have employed a nanny. These employers have to become accustomed to having someone working and perhaps living in their home. The nanny's awareness of potential areas of conflict and willingness to raise issues before they become serious problems is particularly important in this situation. First-time parents have to deal with their feelings about leaving their baby with a caregiver. This transition is usually easier if the nanny begins work while the mother is still on maternity leave.

Communications between the nanny and employers are critical during the orientation period. Do not hesitate to ask for more information if you are not clear about what to do, where things are located, or how to operate equipment. You will earn the confidence of your employers and be able to work unsupervised more quickly if you ask intelligent questions and show a willingness to learn.

Courtesy and tact help make the nanny an asset to the household rather than an intrusion. Other ways to ensure that employers value your entry into their home and lives is to clean up after yourself, treat their possessions with care, offer to pay for anything you break or damage, meet your share of expenses, and not abuse any privileges they extend to you.

Punctuality, neat appearance, initiative, cooperation, and dignity demonstrate a sense of professionalism from the start. It is important for your success as a nanny to begin your job acting as you wish to be perceived by your employers.

The following guidelines are suggested for adapting to your new employers, although details will differ from one work situation to another:

- Ask employers what they prefer you to call them, if you do not already know.

- Review the written employment agreement and nanny's job description with employers.

- Clarify policies on telephone and television use, kitchen privileges, drinking, smoking, space, and curfews (these are usually included in the written agreement, see pages 92 and 93; 172 and 173; also see Appendix A).

- Plan for regular communications: daily logs and reports and weekly nanny/employer conferences (see pages 93 and 94; 95 and 96).

- Find out the family's typical routine, including when employers leave for work and return, family mealtimes, when employers want to settle down at night and not be disturbed, and weekend schedules that may be relevant to the nanny.

- Ask how the employers prefer the telephone to be answered.

- Ask about arrangements for petty cash to be available for emergency expenses and for children's outings.

- Provide your employers with the name, address, and telephone number of the person you wish to be notified in the event you are ill or injured or any other emergency.

The Community

Although your employers may provide you with some information about the new community to help you feel secure and comfortable, you should be prepared to identify what you need and do some of your own research. The following guidelines are suggested:

◆ Contact the Chamber of Commerce for maps and information about community activities, cultural events, and places of interest.

◆ Read the local newspaper to become familiar with your new environment.

◆ If available, read a parenting newspaper to discover places and events of interest to the children in your care.

◆ Obtain a history of the area to understand it better.

◆ Locate the public library, parks, swimming pools, grocery and drug stores, shopping center, movie theater.

◆ Locate the hospital, police station, fire department, post office, city hall.

◆ Contact a new doctor, dentist, or other needed health professional and arrange for your records to be sent from your previous providers.

◆ Locate a new place of worship.

◆ Locate a new bank, dry cleaners, hairdresser, shoe repair.

◆ Contact the YMCA/YWCA or local Board of Education about fitness programs.

MANAGING YOUR TIME

One of your first tasks will be to plan your working hours so you can fulfill the responsibilities listed in your job description and meet the individual needs of the children in your care.

Child care involves many different activities in the course of the working day. Time spent on planning and organization actually saves time. With a plan, you will feel in better control of your day and less likely to experience stress when the unexpected happens—as it often does when working with young children.

In general, child-care activities fall into two groups, (1) activities that take place at predictable times, for example, meals, naps, drop off and pick up at nursery school, daily planned play activities/outings; and (2) activities for which more flexibility is available, for example, unstructured play, folding laundry, organizing the child's clothing and toys, clothing repair, maintaining the child's quarters, running errands. When considering your work plan, first identify and write in the predictable activities and then fit in the other duties to be accomplished. Some tasks can be done while you are doing something else, for example, folding a basket of clean laundry or doing some preliminary lunch preparation when you are in the kitchen supervising a mid-morning snack and interacting with the child. Use a small chunk of time to complete a small task such as sewing on a button or to do part of a big task that can be broken into pieces such as seasonal clothing organization. The nature of child care is such that large portions of uninterrupted time are rarely available and a nanny must become adept at using each minute effectively. Duties may include tasks best done without a child around you. For example, cleaning the children's bathroom can be scheduled for nap time or while a preschooler is at nursery school. When the nursery has a thorough clean, baby can nap in the portable crib or baby carriage in another room or screened-in porch, weather permitting.

Figure 9.1 provides an example of a work plan for a nanny caring for John, age ten months, and Clare, age three years. Clare attends nursery school three mornings a week from 9:00 AM to 11:30 AM. The example describes a nursery school morning with the nanny driving both ways. On the two mornings Clare stays at home, there will be time for an outing or play before John's nap. The nanny will have more time for household tasks later in the morning because Clare does not have to be picked up. Working parents often like to be involved in their children's bath and bedtime routines, and it could be the case that at least one of Clare's and John's parents arrives home by 5:30 PM in time for baths. In that event, the nanny's workday would be shorter. If Clare visits a little friend for the afternoon after nursery school, or grandparents take one or both children for part of the day, the nanny would have an opportunity to do maintenance of children's quarters and equipment that is not easily accomplished within the normal routine. Perhaps closets, chests, and shelves are due

---

A WORK PLAN

7:30   On duty. Children get up. Morning care for John (wash face, hands, diaper area; dress). Assist Clare with washing and dressing. Strip crib, pull back covers on Clare's bed, air bedrooms.

7:45   Breakfast. After breakfast, finish grooming (teeth, hair, etc.). Kitchen clean up. Load washing machine. Children free playtime.

8:40   Prepare both children to drive Clare to school for 9:00.

9:20   Return home. Make bed and crib. Clean/tidy children's bedrooms. John's snack, cuddle time, and nap. Change laundry to dryer. Continue washing machine as necessary. Clean children's bathroom. Start lunch preparations.

11:00   John up. Prepare to pick Clare up at 11:30.

12:00   Lunch for children and nanny. Kitchen clean up. Play and read with children.

1:30   John's nap and Clare's rest time on bed. Nanny uses nap/rest time for ironing, planning menus and children's activities, clothing repairs, starting dinner preparations or similar tasks.

2:30   Clare up. Snack. Fold laundry. Play activities with Clare.

3:30   John up. Snack. Outside play for both children at home or park.

4:30   Prepare children's dinner. Children free playtime.

5:00   Children's dinner. Kitchen clean up. Tidy toys and play-room. Check other play areas and tidy house as needed. Put laundry away.

5:45   Baths. Quiet activity (e.g., music, story) with children until parents arrive. Brief verbal report, transition time.

6:30   Off duty.

Figure 9.1   A work plan.

for more thorough organization than usual. The time might be used to complete a task that was postponed because something unexpected happened. A well-organized nanny is always aware of what needs to be done and welcomes opportunities to catch up or get ahead with duties.

Keep in mind that managing time effectively extends to many aspects of the job and daily life. Learn to estimate with reasonable accuracy how long it will take to do a task or get from one place to another. Underestimating the needed time is a common problem, resulting in stress as you see the clock move toward the hour of your employers' return or the time of an appointment when you are caught in rush-hour traffic. Procrastination is a time waster. Remembering that the gas tank is near empty on a nursery school morning will result in time-wasting anxiety, the child's late arrival and your late return home. Tasks need to be done in a timely way. Whenever possible, tackle jobs you dislike first, so they get done and you will not worry about them all day. Make to-do lists for yourself in personal and professional life. Identify jobs that need to be done first. Lists help ensure that nothing is forgotten and give you a sense of accomplishment when you cross through a completed task.

TRIAL PERIOD

It is not until employment begins that the nanny and employers can get a real sense of whether the arrangement is going to work as anticipated. This is the purpose of the trial period in the written employment agreement (see pages 92 and 93 and Appendix A). Usually two to four weeks in length, the trial period allows either the nanny or the employers to withdraw from the arrangement early on, with the minimum of disruption, especially to the children.

Employment should be started in a positive way and with a willingness to make necessary adjustments. At the end of the trial period, the nanny and family usually initial the employment agreement as evidence of their intention to continue with the arrangement. Sometimes at this point, the nanny and employers agree to some minor changes in the written agreement because the trial period has given them time to see how it works in practice.

If there are questions or problems arising from any aspect of starting a new job, the agency that made the placement should be contacted, or the school that trained the nanny. Their support and advice may be all that is needed to help smooth the transition and make it successful. If, despite the best of efforts, the nanny feels unable to be effective in this position, the nanny should withdraw from the arrangement within the trial period. Once the written work agreement has been affirmed, the nanny should adhere to the commitment described in it (see commitment, pages 153 and 154).

The trial period, or **probation**, as it is sometimes called, gives employers the opportunity to evaluate the nanny on the job before affirming the written work agreement.

BIBLIOGRAPHY

Breese, C., and Gomer, H. (1988). *The Good Nanny Guide*. London, UK: Century Hutchinson, Ltd.

Charlesworth, E., and Nathan, R. (1984). *Stress Management*, Section Six, "Planning Your Days and Your Years." New York: Ballantine Books.

Forney, D. (1986). "Ask Diana." *National Nanny Newsletter* 2(2), 3.

probation—A trial period.

Chapter 10

Leaving a Position

TOPICS

- ◆ Introduction
- ◆ Submitting Your Resignation

- ◆ When the Employer Terminates Employment
- ◆ Leaving the Children

INTRODUCTION

Leaving a position in an appropriate manner is an important part of professionalism. It makes it easier on everyone, especially the children, if the nanny handles departure with sensitivity and dignity. The portion of the written agreement that concerns termination of employment provides a framework for what should be done to end the work arrangement, whether at the nanny's or the employers' initiative. Provisions include the length of notice to be given and any severance pay that will be due.

SUBMITTING YOUR RESIGNATION

When you have decided to leave a position, arrange to meet with your employers at a convenient time so you can give them notice verbally and provide them with a written letter of resignation at the same time. The letter confirms your intention to leave and when you expect your last day of work to be.

The discussion about your departure should be kept as calm and harmonious as possible. This is not the time to air grievances or bargain for improvements in the work arrangement so you will stay. Once you have decided to leave, for whatever reason, focus on making a smooth departure so that your employers and the children are left with positive feelings about the time you spent with them. Reasonable employers do not expect a nanny to stay with them forever. They appreciate the nanny who has kept and very possibly exceeded the commitment to work a certain length of time, but realize that for various reasons nannies move on. If communications between the nanny and employers have been good, the nanny's resignation will be discussed constructively and the parting will be friendly.

Besides giving proper notice and making your intentions clear to your employers, there are several other things you can do to ensure a positive closure to your working relationship with this family. A very important element in this will be dealing with the children's reactions; this is discussed on pages 198 and 199. Once notice has been given, expect a change in your relationship with your employers. Often subtle, this change is part of the adjustment to the prospect of ending the relationship as it now exists. However, it must not be allowed to interfere with the nanny maintaining the highest standards of work during the remaining weeks. Excitement about moving on to whatever lies ahead must not divert the nanny's energy and attention from fulfilling obligations to present employers and children. It is tactless to make enthusiastic references to a new job, for example, or getting married or starting college, particularly in front of the children.

Make sure that anything you have borrowed is returned to employers or other rightful owners. Return library books. Organize any written information you were given or acquired when you were oriented to this job and ask your employers if they would like it for their next nanny. Return keys before leaving.

If you are a live-in nanny and responsible for maintaining your own quarters, clean them thoroughly, including drawers, closets, and bathroom cabinets, in readiness for the new nanny. Let your employers know if there is damage to the walls when pictures are removed and offer to repair it. Put clean linens on the bed and clean towels in the bathroom on the day you leave. If an employer's car has been available for your personal as well as work use, it should be left clean, tidy, and fueled. A departing nanny who is considerate and conscientious to the end maintains the good opinion of employers and smooths the way for the new nanny.

Obtain a reference or letter of recommendation from your employers as soon after giving notice as possible. Promises to mail it later are sometimes forgotten when the family is adjusting to a new nanny.

WHEN THE EMPLOYER TERMINATES EMPLOYMENT

Employers decide to terminate employment for a variety of reasons, just as nannies do. Perhaps the children have outgrown their need for a nanny or parents want to make different child-care arrangements altogether. Perhaps the family is moving and cannot take you with them. Sometimes families, like nannies, are just ready for a change. Whatever the reason, it is important to keep your professional poise, even when termination comes as a surprise. If there is criticism of your work, accepting it constructively is more likely to earn you a fair and helpful reference than becoming angry and argumentative.

Whatever the circumstances of termination are, the nanny must maintain a professional attitude toward employers, children, and responsibilities during the remaining days of employment. Steps for smoothing the nanny's departure and transition for the family that were described in the previous section (pages 196–197) should be followed in this situation. A reference or letter of recommendation should be obtained before departure.

Occasionally, a nanny is dismissed or asked to leave without notice. Difficult though it may be, the nanny must act professionally while arranging to leave as soon as possible. Any severance pay due should be collected before leaving and may be necessary for the nanny's travel expenses home or elsewhere.

In some circumstances, a nanny who has been terminated may be eligible for unemployment benefits. Inquiry should be made at a State Bureau of Employment Services in the state where the nanny was employed.

LEAVING THE CHILDREN

From the start of a job, a nanny knows that caring for this particular child will end some day. The nanny recognizes the primary place of parents in the child's life and accepts the temporary nature of the nanny/child relationship. Although feelings of sadness at leaving a child are understandable, it is neither professional nor helpful to the child for the nanny to indulge in emotional displays.

It is important to maintain normal routines for the child who is facing the departure of a caregiver with whom a warm attachment has been formed. A good nanny prepares the child for the separation to come. In a way appropriate to the age of the child, you should explain where you are going and when you will be leaving. If you can visit, tell the child when you will do so, but do not make a promise you cannot keep. Arrangements to visit should be made with the approval of the child's parents.

It is difficult for a child to understand why a nanny has left. Parents should not become so occupied with finding and orienting a new caregiver that they overlook or minimize a child's distress.

Sending a child postcards and making occasional telephone calls can help ease the transition for the child and reassure her of your ongoing affection. However, be careful not to compete with the relationship the child is developing with the new nanny.

For many nannies, maintaining enduring friendships with the children they have cared for and with parents is one of the rewards of the job.

BIBLIOGRAPHY

Breese, C., and Gomer, H. (1988). *The Good Nanny Guide*. London, UK: Century Hutchinson, Ltd.

Forney, D. (1987). "How to Leave a Job." *Nanny Handbook: Essays from the National Nanny Newsletter*. Claremont, CA: International Nanny Association.

Magagna, J. (1986). "Aspects of the mother/nanny relationship: Some concepts from analytic research to understand problems which can interfere with the optimal care for children." Paper delivered at the International Nanny Conference, August 1986, Scripps College, Claremont, CA.

Chapter 11

Special Situations

TOPICS

- ◆ Introduction
- ◆ Child Abuse and Neglect
- ◆ Domestic Violence
- ◆ Drug Abuse
- ◆ Sexual Harassment

Terms to Know

child abuse
child neglect
socioeconomic
mandated
behavior
skeletal
laceration
abrasion
Shaken Baby Syndrome
regression

bulimia
anorexia nervosa
hives
facial tics
failure to thrive
ethnic
sex role
fetal alcohol syndrome
paraphernalia

INTRODUCTION

This chapter examines difficult situations that may be encountered while working with children and parents in a private home. A nanny needs to be aware of indications that a family or a family member is not functioning properly and know the appropriate action to take.

CHILD ABUSE AND NEGLECT

What would you do if you knew or suspected that:

◆ A baby had been left in a locked car on a 90-degree day?

◆ A four-year old had been sexually abused by the substitute babysitter?

◆ A parent failed to send a child to school regularly or seek medical treatment for the child when necessary?

◆ The burns or bruises on the child were deliberately inflicted?

◆ A child is constantly subjected to ridicule and shame?

These are all examples of **child abuse** and **neglect**. Most victims are very young children who cannot talk or do not know how to get help. Abuse and neglect happen in many kinds of families and in every community. Children who are abused or neglected cannot be identified by racial, ethnic, religious, or **socioeconomic** class.

A nanny must be alert to protect children. Many professionals—such as child-care providers, teachers, physicians, nurses, social workers, clergy, and others whose work brings them in contact with children and families—are **mandated** by state law to report suspected abuse or neglect, or be subject to penalties if they fail to report and a child is later harmed. Nannies should find out what their legal responsibilities are for reporting in the state where they are working. This may be done by contacting the local county welfare department. In addition to any legal responsibility, *a nanny has a professional and moral responsibility to report suspected abuse or neglect.*

Defining Child Abuse and Neglect

Child abuse and neglect take many forms. A key element in recognizing when a child is being mistreated is a basic understanding of the terms abuse and neglect. There are several factors involved in defining abuse and neglect, including cultural and ethnic backgrounds, attitudes related to parenting, and professional training. Varying views are held on when discipline and punishment become abuse or neglect. For example, at what point does spanking become abuse? Federal legislation requires states to establish definitions, policies, procedures, and laws with regard to child abuse and neglect.

---

child abuse—Physical, emotional, or sexual mistreatment of a child.

child neglect—Failure of a parent or guardian to meet a child's basic needs.

socioeconomic—Involving both social and economic factors.

mandated—Required, ordered.

Abuse represents an action against a child—something that is done to a child that ought not to be done and includes physical, emotional, and sexual abuse.

Physical abuse includes the nonaccidental injury or death of a child, putting a child's health and safety at substantial risk (for example, leaving a child alone in a locked car), cruelty to a child, and harsh, prolonged punishment that creates a substantial risk of serious harm to a child, including physical restraint (for example, tying a child down in a crib).

More difficult to recognize than physical abuse, *emotional abuse* covers repeated acts that interfere with a child's social and psychological development. Even the best of parents may lose control and shout at a child or be overly critical on occasion, but when a child constantly hears that she is no good, cannot do anything right or is stupid, or is threatened with withdrawal of love, the child's self-esteem and ability to trust others will be affected. The results of emotional abuse may not become apparent until adolescence or later.

Sexual abuse includes any act of a sexual nature between an adult and a child, regardless of whether the child agreed to participate. The act may be for the sexual gratification of the perpetrator or a third party and includes anyone who allowed or encouraged the sexual activity, as well as the active participant. Sexual abuse has long-term consequences for the victim if it goes undetected and untreated. Boys, as well as girls, can be victims of sexual abuse.

Neglect represents childrearing practices that are inadequate or dangerous. Put another way, neglect is the failure to provide the things a child needs to grow up healthy and safe, such as supervision, shelter, food, clothing, medical attention, and education. It also covers failure to provide the affection and support necessary for a child's social and psychological development.

A child for purposes of protection under abuse and neglect laws is someone who is under 18 years of age, or under 21 years of age if physically or mentally handicapped.

The perpetrator of abuse or neglect can be anyone who has care or control of a child at the relevant time, for example: parent, guardian, foster parent, teacher, family friend, relative, caregiver, bus driver, or playground attendant. The perpetrator is more likely to be someone the child knows rather than a stranger.

Abuse and neglect usually result from a complex combination of human factors and circumstances. There are no simple explanations for why parents or other adults entrusted with children's well-being would mistreat them. A parent or caretaker with inadequate coping skills may abuse a child when a crisis or environmental stress occurs. The crisis may be apparently trivial in nature, such as a flat tire, spilled milk, a child's persistent crying, or wet pants. It may be a difficult event in family life, such as the loss of a job, marital problems, illness, or death. The significance of the crisis is not its severity, but the situation it creates for the abuser, who is unable to cope with frustration and stress in a normal manner. Some adults have inappropriate concepts of discipline. They may be unaware of appropriate behavior for a child at a given age. For example, they may expect the 12-month-old to be toilet-trained or the 16-month-old to eat without making a mess. The likelihood of abuse or neglect increases when adults have severe personal problems such as drug addiction or alcoholism. Immaturity, unwillingness to accept the demands of childrearing, or ignorance of a child's physical or emotional needs can lead to abuse or neglect. Abusive or neglectful parents were often victims of the same kind of parenting they provide for their children.

Recognizing Abuse and Neglect

There are two basic types of clues to abuse and neglect, physical and behavioral. The child's appearance or evidence of injuries provides obvious physical indicators of abuse or neglect. More difficult to identify and interpret than physical indicators, extremes of **behavior** or changes in behavior may indicate abuse or neglect.

---

behavior—Anything that a person does or says that can be observed.

Awareness of clues to abuse and neglect enables nannies to intervene on a child's behalf. Unrecognized, abuse or neglect can continue for a long time because a child does not reveal the problem for various reasons. He may not understand that what is happening to him is abnormal, or he may believe it is his fault. Abusers use threats and tricks to keep the abuse a secret. Fear of the abuser often keeps a child silent, or he may be afraid of what will happen to his family if he tells. Unless the physical trauma is discovered, sexual abuse is particularly difficult to detect. Behavioral clues may be the best or only indicators of the problem.

Keep in mind that some behaviors can be normal for a given child at a given time. It is important to be aware of new behaviors, extreme behaviors, or a combination of indicators, both physical and behavioral, that suggest abuse or neglect.

Indicators of Physical Abuse

- ◆ Evidence of repeated injuries
- ◆ Bruises in various stages of healing
- ◆ Marks in the shape of the instrument used
- ◆ Bilateral and/or clustered injuries
- ◆ Unexplained burns
- ◆ Unexplained **skeletal** injuries such as injuries from severe twisting, pulling, or striking an arm or leg
- ◆ Other unexplained or repeated injuries such as **lacerations**, **abrasions**, welts, scars, injuries to and around the mouth, loss of hair, eye injury, abdominal injury
- ◆ Signs of head/neck injury in an infant (**Shaken Baby Syndrome**)

---

skeletal—*Pertaining to the body's bony framework, the skeleton.*

laceration—*A wound or irregular tear of the skin or other tissue.*

abrasion—*Superficial injury to skin or mucous membrane from scraping or rubbing.*

Shaken Baby Syndrome—*Head injury in an infant resulting from forceful shaking.*

◆ Injuries inconsistent with the child's developmental stage, such as bruises on an infant

◆ Efforts to hide injuries or explain them in ways that are inconsistent or unbelievable

◆ Extremes of behavior such as withdrawal, aggression, or **regression**

◆ Fear of a parent or caretaker

◆ Unusual shyness, resistance to physical contact

◆ Frequent complaints of pain

◆ Excessive crying

◆ Antisocial behavior such as truancy, running away, drug use

Indicators of Emotional Abuse

◆ Developmental delays in speech or motor skills

◆ Speech disorders such as stammering

◆ Eating disorders such as obesity, **bulimia, anorexia nervosa**

◆ Frequent vomiting

◆ Nervous disorders such as **hives, facial tics**, or stomachache

◆ Flat or bald spots on an infant's head

---

regression—*A return to an earlier stage of development in response to a stressful situation.*

bulimia—*Eating disorder characterized by secretive bingeing (rapid overeating) and purging (such as self-induced vomiting or use of laxatives and enemas).*

anorexia nervosa—*Eating disorder characterized by self-imposed starvation and persistent denial of any appetite for food.*

hives—*Eruption or itchy wheals on the skin caused by reaction to an allergic substance in food, medication, or by direct skin contact.*

facial tic—*Minor involuntary muscular movement or twitching of face that may be associated with a psychological factor.*

- Nonorganic **failure to thrive** in infants
- Regressive behavior
- Habit disorders such as head banging, rocking, or biting
- Rarely smiles or laughs
- Lack of spontaneity, creativity
- Behavioral extremes: very compliant or demanding; withdrawn or aggressive; listless or excitable
- Poor relationships with peers
- Behavior that is either too adult or infantile for age
- Detached, given to excessive daydreaming or fantasizing
- Enjoys inflicting pain on others or being mistreated
- Fire-setting

Indicators of Sexual Abuse

- Torn, stained, or bloody underclothing
- Bruises or bleeding from external genitalia, vagina, or anal region
- Pain, itching, swelling in genital area; difficulty in walking
- Genital discharge
- Sexually transmitted disease
- Frequent, unexplained sore throats, yeast infections, urinary tract infections
- Sudden changes in behavior
- Regressive behavior
- Nightmares
- Reluctance to undress or wants to wear extra layers of clothes
- Inability to relate to other children of own age

---

failure to thrive—Malnourished, underweight condition of infancy; many causes, but often associated with inadequate feeding and stimulation.

- In young children, preoccupation with sexual organs of self, parents, or other children
- Age-inappropriate ways of displaying affection
- Decline in school performance, truancy
- Delinquency, seductive behavior, promiscuity, drug abuse
- Pregnancy
- Child may disclose sexual abuse

Indicators of Neglect

- Poor hygiene; bad odor from unwashed body, hair, clothes
- Severe or untreated diaper rash
- Failure to thrive in infants
- Untreated illness or injury; lack of dental care or immunizations
- Clothing unsuitable for the weather, or too large or small for child
- Height and weight significantly low for age
- Excessive sunburn, insect bites, colds, or other indications of prolonged outdoor exposure
- Chronic hunger or tiredness
- May beg for or steal food
- Dull, apathetic appearance
- Spends time alone; has difficulty getting along with other children
- May assume adult responsibilities
- Delinquency, vandalism, drug abuse
- May report no caretaker at home

Especially Vulnerable Children

A child who is perceived to be different or who does not measure up to certain expectations may be singled out for abuse. These include children who are handicapped, physically unattractive, fussy, hyperactive, very timid or weak, or similar to someone the perpetrator dislikes. Children who are stepchildren, under three years of age, or born from unwanted or unplanned pregnancies are at increased risk of becoming victims.

Characteristics of Abusive or Neglectful Adults

In addition to observing the child, awareness of common characteristics of abusive or neglectful adults can be helpful in identifying a situation where there is abuse or neglect. Adults may share several of the following characteristics:

- Isolation from family supports such as friends, relatives, neighbors and community groups; rarely participate in social or school activities.

- Overcritical of child and seldom speak of him in positive terms; seldom look at or touch child.

- Inappropriate response to the child's condition, either by overreacting or becoming hostile when questioned, or underreacting, showing indifference and appearing more concerned about their own problems than those of the child.

- Poor self-concept; perceive themselves as unlovable, worthless.

- Lack of parenting skills and show little understanding of a child's developmental needs and how to meet them; place unrealistic demands on the child and see the child's inability to perform as deliberate disobedience.

- Impulsive behavior, crave excitement and change, impatient.

- Unmet emotional needs; cannot give warmth and love to a child; look to the child for their emotional fulfillment.

- Unable to form successful interpersonal relationships for socializing and working together.

- Violence accepted as a means of communication.

- Marital difficulties; passive marital relationship; abusive spouse.

◆ Misuse of alcohol, drugs.

◆ Abused or neglected as a child.

If a Child Tells You about Abuse or Neglect

A child may share the secret of abuse of neglect either directly or indirectly. A child is demonstrating her trust in you by taking you into her confidence. She is also showing courage, because it is not easy to tell and she may have many fears about the consequences.

Listen carefully to what the child tells you, without making assumptions or projecting your own thoughts. Listen in an accepting way and do not press the child for details or ask for more information than she wants to reveal. Reassure the child that she has done the right thing in telling and she is in no way to blame for the abuse or neglect. Commend her for telling.

Although it may be a difficult situation for you, keep your feelings under control no matter how angry or repelled you may feel. Remain calm, nonjudgmental and uncritical of the child's family. Allow the child to use her own vocabulary to describe what happened even though the terms the child uses make you uncomfortable.

It is important not to make promises you cannot keep. You cannot promise not to tell. Explain honestly that this is a problem you cannot handle yourself, but that there are people ready to help. Assess the child's immediate safety. If there is a crisis situation, contact the local police department.

Reporting Suspected Abuse and Neglect

Prompt reporting protects the child and enables troubled families to get the help they need. Society also benefits from child protection. Studies have linked child abuse and neglect to a wide range of criminal and antisocial behaviors as victims grow up, including an ongoing cycle of abuse and neglect as victims become perpetrators.

The reporter need only suspect that a child is being mistreated or inadequately cared for to contact child protective services. It is the responsibility of the agency to gather additional information from various sources and determine if a situation of abuse or neglect exists. If you are not sure what to do, contact child protective services with your concerns anyway. Keep in mind that *silence is the ally of the abuser* and it is always better to decide in favor of protecting a child.

Usually the initial report is made by telephone. Mandated reporters are usually asked for a followup written report. Nannies should have their local child-abuse telephone number available. Children's protective services usually come under the county social services/welfare department. Reports can also be made to the police.

Information that is usually given in the report includes: the child's name, address, and age; name(s) and address of the parent(s) or guardian; the reasons to believe the child is being abused or neglected (injuries, other signs of abuse or neglect; evidence of previous abuse or neglect); the identity of the suspected perpetrator and address if known, and any other information that may assist the investigation. Even if all this information is not available, the report should still be made.

As long as the report is made in good faith, state laws protect the reporter from liability. However, suspicions of abuse and neglect should be handled in a professional way and not discussed carelessly. The identity of the reporter is kept confidential except by express order of the court.

In order to avoid putting the child in additional danger, suspicions of abuse or neglect should not be discussed with the suspected family or individual. Suspicions should be reported promptly and the child's safety assured. The decision whether to inform the family or individual later about the report depends on the particular circumstances.

It is not easy to report an employer, colleague, neighbor, relative, or acquaintance, but as advocates for children, nannies must help to protect them. Furthermore, the intent of reporting laws is not to punish families in trouble, but to work with them so they can take better care of their children.

Nannies Working with Children and Families

As a professional who cares about children and families, you may identify early indications of a potentially abusive situation. You should become aware of community resources that are available to families facing a particularly stressful time and in need of support or services (see Appendix F). A trusting relationship between the nanny and family enables concerns to be shared. Let parents know if you observe signs of stress in the child. Always model appropriate childrearing techniques and share your knowledge of child development in tactful ways when there are particular childrearing issues to be discussed. Your early and sensitive intervention could prevent harm to a child and disruption to a family.

Another important aspect of prevention is teaching children personal safety skills. This includes teaching them how to recognize uncomfortable situations, when to tell a trusted adult, how to say "no" if someone tries to do something inappropriate, and letting them know it is not normal and they do not deserve to be mistreated, forced into sexual activity, or left alone for long periods of time. Methods and materials for educating children about personal safety, particularly with respect to sexual abuse prevention, must be developmentally appropriate and not foster misunderstanding or fear about acceptable touching, normal sexual activity, having a doctor check "private parts," or trust in adults.

In September 1996, the National Association for the Education of Young Children (NAEYC) adopted a position statement on "The Prevention of Child Abuse in Early Childhood Programs and the Responsibilities of Early Childhood Professionals to Prevent Child Abuse." The statement recommends policies and procedures for protecting children in child care. For further information, NAEYC may be contacted at 1-800-424-2460.

The National Committee to Prevent Child Abuse offers many inexpensive publications for parents and professionals. A free catalog may be obtained by calling 1-800-499-6464. In some communities, Child Assault Prevention (CAP) programs, developed by the National Center for Assault Prevention, may be available.

CAP programs involve parents, teachers, and other concerned adults in sexual abuse prevention. Books about child abuse and additional resources are suggested in Appendices D and E respectively.

Since abuse is such a sensitive and emotional issue, a nanny needs to discuss it openly with parents. It is important for the nanny to know how parents have approached the issue to protect their children and if there have been any problems in the past. This can be an appropriate topic to include in health and safety concerns during the interview process. Unwillingness on the part of one or both parents to discuss the topic would be a consideration in deciding whether to take the position.

Another concern for nannies is the possibility of being unjustly accused of abusing a child. It is reassuring to parents if they know the nanny they are hiring has a clean criminal record. This should be part of pre-employment screening (see page 156). Having a written job description, keeping a daily log that includes all injuries and incidents, and contacting parents during the day if there are special concerns all help to protect the nanny against accusations of causing any harm to the child. Open, honest discussion of every issue related to the child's well-being also helps to build an effective working relationship based on trust.

A nanny must *never* use physical or emotional punishment. Discuss discipline and let parents know where you stand during the interview process, before you even accept a position.

Injuries and incidents that happened while you were off duty should be documented. Ask parents what happened and make a note of it if you observe an injury when you come back to work. It is always important to distinguish between what happened when the child was in your care and when in the care of someone else. If abuse is occurring, the record will be useful in identifying a pattern of suspicious events and help to protect you from being blamed. Changes in the child's behavior should also be documented.

If you have reason to suspect abuse, report your suspicions to children's protective services or, if you are not sure what to do, call and ask for advice. The consequence of reporting abuse involving an employer or an employer's relative or friend may be the loss of your job, but your responsibility to the child must be the primary consideration. If you find yourself in a difficult situation, several agencies offer assistance with legal and other questions related to abuse and sexual assault (see Appendix D).

DOMESTIC VIOLENCE

Domestic violence refers to the violent behavior of one partner toward the other partner in an intimate relationship. Besides physical abuse, domestic violence may include sexual violence and psychological abuse, such as threats, intimidation and isolation. Also referred to as spouse abuse, domestic violence applies not only to wives and husbands, but to girlfriends and boyfriends, and partners in other forms of intimate relationships.

Although men may be victims of domestic violence, it is rare. The problems of domestic violence are generally considered to be those of violence toward women. A man usually does not have physical and economic constraints to keep him in an abusive relationship as is commonly the case for a woman. Nor does he usually require a community shelter to protect him from further danger. This section, therefore, examines wife abuse, or wife battering, which includes the mistreatment of a woman by a husband, former husband, or male companion. Like child abuse, wife abuse occurs everywhere, among families of all **ethnic** backgrounds, religions and incomes.

Conflict and stress occur normally in any close, intimate relationship. As a nanny, you may well become aware of angry arguments or a strained atmosphere between your employers from time to time. This may be distressing to you, particularly if you grew up in a home where voices were rarely raised. Normal "family fights" are none of the nanny's business. The nanny should remain neutral and out of the way. On the other hand,

---

ethnic—*Pertaining to a group of people distinguished by a common history, customs, language, and other shared characteristics.*

wife abuse involves physical contact with intent to harm and it is a crime. Besides slaps and punches, a dangerous weapon such as a heavy object, a knife, or a gun may be involved.

Wife abuse affects the whole family. The physical harm to the victim can be very serious, sometimes fatal. Emotional damage occurs, too. Besides living in fear of attack, the victim commonly takes responsibility for provoking the violence even though she has done nothing wrong. Feelings of guilt, shame, and failure prevent a woman from doing anything about the situation. The longer she accepts it, the more these feelings are reinforced.

Children are harmed when they live with domestic violence. They may be victims of abuse themselves. Even if they are not physically hurt, they suffer emotional damage. As they grow up, they may become violent adults or victims of domestic violence. In pregnancy, the fetus can be harmed or a miscarriage precipitated by wife abuse.

Abusers may experience guilt and shame, but are unable to control their violent outbursts. Some become victims of violence themselves when an abused woman finally strikes back and kills her abuser. Abusers usually appear to be nice, ordinary people, but they possess hidden emotional problems that find an outlet in wife abuse. Common characteristics of abusers include growing up in a violent home (either as a witness to or a victim of violence), low self-esteem, and poor communication skills. A sense of underachievement in the breadwinner role may be present. The woman becomes the target when feelings of resentment and anger are released. The misuse of alcohol or other drugs is sometimes a factor in abuse. Cultural attitudes toward the **sex roles** and society's tolerance of violence as a way to resolve conflict may play a part. As in the case of child abuse, the cause of wife abuse is complex. The lowest incidence of marital violence is seen in families where decision making is shared by the husband and wife.

Episodes of abuse usually follow a pattern. Tension builds over a small incident or series of incidents, such as an unacceptable

---

sex role—*societal or cultural characteristics (masculine or feminine) of one's gender.*

meal, a request for money, a purchase, or disagreement over which television show to watch. The tension erupts into violence. Once the attack has begun, nothing the victim says or does can stop it. After the attack is over, the abuser typically becomes remorseful and affectionate, promising never to hurt his wife again. He may really intend to keep his promise and the wife wants to believe him. However, as tension builds again, battering will be repeated. Most abuse happens when there are no witnesses.

Typically the woman explains her injuries to friends, emergency room staff and others as accidental. Even if she or someone else calls the police, she does not press charges against the abuser. Many women remain caught in a cycle of violence for years. Experience has taught them that resistance or complaints only lead to more or worse violence. They often fear for their lives. Low self-esteem, hope that the man may change, or a reluctance to reveal a perceived failure as a wife and mother are among the reasons women stay in abusive situations. Other reasons can include a woman's economic dependence on her husband, a belief that divorce is wrong or that children should have a father in the home under any circumstances, or pressure from relatives and friends to preserve the marriage. As a child, a woman may have seen her mother submit to years of abuse from her father.

What Can Be Done

First, an abused woman has to acknowledge to herself that she is being abused and that this is not right or fair. She needs to talk to those who can help. Confiding in a trusted friend or relative, or consulting a counselor can be the first step toward ending the problem and starting a new life. A nanny might offer support and guidance by suggesting organizations whose purpose it is to assist women in bad situations, such as emergency shelters, hotlines, social service agencies, or mental health centers. An abused woman needs to find out what her options are and make her own decision about what to do. With counseling for herself and her husband, a woman may be able to remain in the marriage and improve it. When there are children, counseling may be appropriate to help them understand the situation and learn that violence is unacceptable. Alternatively, a woman may decide to build a better life for herself and her children by leaving the marriage. This usually involves seeking temporary housing and practical help at a women's emergency shelter. More information about state and local resources for abused women may be obtained from: National Coalition Against Domestic Violence, 1728 N Street, N.W., Washington, DC 20036.

In an Emergency

An abused woman should be prepared for emergency action when an attack is likely or when one occurs. This includes having an escape plan for herself and her children so they can reach a shelter or the home of a trusted relative or friend. Telephone numbers for the police and wife abuse hotline should be at hand. Car keys, money, and important documents such as birth certificates and medical records should be kept in a safe but accessible place.

A victim or a witness of an attack should call the police immediately. It is important to obtain the names and badge numbers of the officers who respond, in the event criminal charges are lodged against the abuser. Medical attention should always be sought following an attack. Injuries may be more severe than they appear at first. In the event of criminal charges, a record of injuries, including photographs, provide additional legal protection.

Domestic violence is not a problem that is easily resolved. Nannies have to recognize their limitations in helping serious, perhaps dangerous, family situations. A nanny should be aware of the resources available to troubled families, in the event an employer or colleague needs assistance (see Appendix F). If abuse is known or suspected, a nanny may be able to persuade the victim to seek professional help. This type of situation is not conducive to a successful, happy job experience. Employers' problems that impact significantly on the nanny are valid reasons for leaving a position. As always, this must be done with the minimum of disruption to the children.

DRUG ABUSE

Widespread abuse of alcohol and other drugs is a matter of deep concern in the United States today. Nannies need to be aware of the problem, how it impacts on families, and what can be done to prevent it in children.

Alcohol Abuse

Alcohol is the most commonly abused drug in the United States. Alcohol abuse can become a chronic, progressive, and potentially fatal illness called alcoholism. Occurring among people of all socioeconomic levels, alcohol abuse has a profound effect on family relationships and job productivity. It has been implicated in motor vehicle and other accidents, child and wife abuse, violent crimes, and fire losses. A child of an alcoholic parent has an increased risk of becoming addicted to alcohol or other drugs.

Excessive alcohol consumption affects the whole family. The alcohol abuser typically denies the problem, blames others, and invents stories to keep the problem a secret and protect him- or herself from criticism. Money is spent on alcohol instead of family needs and debts accumulate. Verbal or physical abuse may be used against the spouse, children, and others. Physical health, personal hygiene, and attention to appearance deteriorate. Feelings of despair and helplessness are experienced and suicide may be attempted.

The spouse or partner commonly contributes to the denial and concealment of the problem. She or he often assumes the responsibilities of the alcohol abuser. A wife may take a job to provide some escape from the problem and achieve financial security. Children may be overprotected, neglected, or used for emotional support. The spouse or partner may turn to alcohol or other drugs to cope with the situation.

Alcohol can harm a child before birth. When alcohol is abused in pregnancy, a child may be born with a pattern of physical, mental, and behavioral abnormalities referred to as **fetal alcohol syndrome**. A child growing up in a home where alcohol is

fetal alcohol syndrome—Birth defects resulting from excessive maternal drinking during pregnancy. Defects may include small head, small eyes, delayed development, and abnormalities of joints, limbs, or organs such as the heart. Also referred to as FAS.

abused is typically deprived of adequate parenting, which leads to a diminished sense of self-worth, avoidance of social activities with peers because of fear and shame, and a loss of trust in adults. Destructive and negative ways of dealing with problems are learned from parents who also fail to provide values and standards for their children.

Abuse of Other Drugs

Besides alcohol, legally available drugs that may be abused include both prescribed and over-the-counter medications (common examples are tranquilizers and medications for sleep and weight control). Illegal drugs include marijuana, cocaine/"crack", heroin, hallucinogens (such as LSD or PCP), and designer drugs. With respect to the consequences for individuals and families, this kind of drug abuse has much in common with alcohol abuse. Serious, sometimes fatal health problems, reduced ability to handle home and work responsibilities, poor parenting, and financial decline as money goes to support the habit are common. There may be participation in criminal activities to maintain a supply of drugs.

What Can Be Done

Whether it is a drinking problem or some other form of drug abuse, the first step to recovery is the acknowledgment that a problem exists. Typically, the spouse or partner of the abuser has to take this first step and get help for him- or herself. Many services and programs are available for assistance, support, and referral, including the local public health department, hospital-based chemical dependency programs, the local council on alcoholism (an affiliate of the National Council on Alcoholism), mental health services, Alcoholics Anonymous (AA), and Al-Anon (for families of alcohol abusers). If the situation is complicated by wife or child abuse, these problems must be addressed through the appropriate agencies.

Children and Drug Abuse

Experimentation with alcohol and other drugs is common among teenagers, but the age at which children have their first drug experience has been decreasing steadily in recent years. Most young people experiment and then stop or use only occasionally without significant problems. Others become regular users with physical, emotional, and social consequences of varying severity. Some develop a dependency with destructive results that may include death. Children with a family history of alcohol or other drug problems are more at risk of developing a problem than other children. Young people who smoke and drink at an early age are at high risk of advancing to marijuana and other illegal drugs.

Warning signs of drug abuse in children include:

◆ Decline in school performance and attendance.

◆ Mood swings that are more pronounced than those typical of adolescents.

◆ Discipline problems; hostile, uncooperative.

◆ Changes in friends, evasive about new ones.

◆ Deterioration in interpersonal relationships with other family members; increasingly argumentative or withdrawn.

◆ Diminished interest in activities that were previously enjoyed.

◆ Increased interest in the drug culture as evidenced by drug literature and **paraphernalia**, and clothing and music with a drug theme.

◆ Changes in eating and sleeping patterns, unusual fatigue, red and dull eyes, coughing, frequent health complaints.

◆ Indifference to personal hygiene and grooming.

These signs may indicate abuse of alcohol or other drugs, or they may be the result of other problems. In any event, parents should have the child examined by a physician to rule out illness

---

paraphernalia—*Drug supplies and equipment, such as pipes, cigarette papers, roach clips, aerosol cans, pills, powder, crushed brown leaves, capsules, glue tubes, beer or liquor containers.*

or other conditions. Following this, comprehensive assessment and drug treatment may be recommended. Family physicians, pediatricians, local hospitals, mental health centers, or school drug programs can assist with appropriate referrals.

Prevention

A warm, trusting relationship with parents and other care-givers provides children with the base for drug education during early childhood and later. Although preschoolers are not ready to learn specific facts about alcohol and other drugs, they can begin to develop the decision-making and problem-solving skills they will need later in life when confronted with pressure to use drugs. A helpful resource for parents, nannies, and others involved with children of all ages is a free handbook available from the United States Department of Education. Entitled *Growing Up Drug Free—A Parent's Guide to Prevention*, the handbook outlines what children at various stages of development should know about drugs and suggests family activities to reinforce children's motivation to avoid alcohol and other drugs. The handbook con-

Figure 11.1 Drug abuse education must be developmentally appropriate and begins with warm, trusting relationships between the child and caring adults.

tains much additional information to enable adults to approach the subject knowledgeably, including resources for more information and help. The guide may be obtained by calling the Department of Education at 1-800-624-0100 (in the Washington, DC area, call 732-3627) or by sending your name and address to: *Growing Up Drug Free*, Pueblo, CO 81009.

Drug abuse prevention is a subject for nannies and parents to discuss as part of a wide range of concerns about children's health, safety, and childrearing practices in general. Modeling the behavior wanted from children is a critical element in teaching children healthy, safe habits. Refraining from tobacco use, using prescribed over-the-counter medications with respect and restraint, and responsible social drinking if alcohol is used at all, are among the ways to model desirable behavior. Responsible social drinking includes knowing what your limit is and adhering to it (individual limits vary and should be discussed with a physician), demonstrating to children that alcohol is not essential for having fun, not pressuring others to drink, not voicing the need for a drink because of a difficult day, not operating a motor vehicle or other machine after drinking, and never treating drunkenness as a joke.

SEXUAL HARASSMENT

Employment in a private home sometimes exposes a nanny to sexual harassment, creating a work environment that is uncomfortable, intimidating and interferes with job performance. Sexual harassment comes in many forms, such as jokes with implicit or explicit sexual connotation, suggestive comments, requests for sexual favors, or actual physical assault. It may involve the conduct of a person of either gender against a person of the opposite or same gender. Sexual harassment is not about sexual or romantic interest, but about the abuse of one person's power and authority over another.

Sexual harassment is a form of sexual discrimination and is prohibited by law. However, federal law applies only to workplaces with 15 or more employers. Individual state law may apply to situations with fewer employees, but a nanny will not be protected unless the household staff is large enough to meet the requirement.

If you are subjected to sexual harassment, you should confront the offender immediately and tell him or her that you are offended by the behavior. *Be direct* and advise the offender that you do not like what was said or done and it must not happen again. Remember, speak up immediately and be very clear in voicing your objections. Confidential written notes about the incident, including time, place, and any witnesses may be useful if harassment persists.

If the problem is not resolved with the offender, the nanny has to decide whether to complain to an employer. If the offender is the other spouse, the nanny may not be believed. The nanny's complaint may or may not be heard more openmindedly if the offender is a relative or a family friend. Again, the nanny has to decide what to do, depending on the particular situation.

If there is no resolution to the problem, a nanny's best protection is to resign in a professional manner. Organizations to contact for more information about sexual harassment or for legal advice are listed in Appendix D.

BIBLIOGRAPHY

American Academy of Pediatrics (1988). *Alcohol: Your Child and Drugs* (brochure). Elk Grove Village, IL: American Academy of Pediatrics.

Channing L. Bete Co., Inc. (1979). *About Wife Abuse.* South Deerfield, MA: Channing L. Bete Co. Inc.

Congressional Research Service (May 7, 1993). *Sexual Harassment: A History of Federal Law.* Washington, DC: Library of Congress.

Congressional Research Service (April 10, 1992). *Family Violence: Background Issues, and the State and Federal Response.* Washington, DC: Library of Congress.

Congressional Research Service (March 9, 1993). *Health Care Fact Sheet: Alcohol Use in the U.S.* Washington, DC: Library of Congress.

Congressional Research Service (March 9, 1993). *Health Care Fact Sheet: Illicit Drug Use in the U.S.* Washington, DC: Library of Congress.

Congressional Quarterly. "Child Sexual Abuse." *CQ Researcher,* January 15, 1993, 25–27.

ERIC Digest. "Child Sexual Abuse: What it is and How to Prevent It." Urbana, IL: ERIC/EECE.

Furman, E. (1987). "More Protections, Fewer Directions: Some Experiences With Helping Children Prevent Sexual Abuse." *Young Children,* 42(5), 5–7. Washington, DC: National Association for the Education of Young Children.

Gelb, L. (1983). *Plain Talk About Wife Abuse.* Washington, DC: U.S. Department of Health and Human Services, Pub. No. ADM-1265.

Goleman, D. "Sexual Harassment: It's about power, not lust." New York Times, October 22, 1991, C1, C12.

Jordan, N.H. (1993). "Sexual Abuse Programs in Early Childhood Education: A Caveat." *Young Children,* 48(6), 76–79. Washington, DC: National Association for the Education of Young Children.

Kendrick, S.K., Kaufman, R. and Messenger, K.P. (Editors) (1991). *Healthy Young Children.* Washington, DC: National Association for the Education of Young Children.

Mikkelsen, E.J. (1997). "Responding to Allegations of Sexual Abuse in Child Care and Early Education Programs." *Young Children,* 52(3), 47–51. Washington, DC: National Association for the Education of Young Children.

"NAEYC Position Statement on the Prevention of Child Abuse in Early Childhood Programs and the Responsibilities of Early Childhood Professionals." (Adopted September 1996). *Young Children,* 52(3), 42–46. Washington, DC: National Association for the Education of Young Children.

National Institute of Justice. "The Cycle of Violence." Research in Brief, October 1992. Washington, DC: U.S. Department of Justice.

Ohio Department of Human Services (1990). *Child Abuse and Neglect*. Columbus, OH: ODHS/Office of Compliance and Review, Pub. No. 1495.

U.S. Department of Education (1990). *Growing Up Drug-Free—A Parent's Guide to Prevention*. Washington, DC: U.S. Government Printing Office.

U.S. Department of Education (1989). *Schools Without Drugs*. Washington, DC: U.S. Department of Education.

Sample Nanny Employment Agreement

This agreement is between _____,
social security number _____,
address: _____ ("Nanny")
and _____,
address: _____ ("Employer").

Employer is hiring Nanny to provide full time child-care
services for _____ (the "Children") as set forth
herein, subject to amendments in writing from time to time:

1. A. Employment shall begin on _____ and
    shall continue until terminated by either party. At this time,
    the parties contemplate that employment will continue at
    least one year.

    B. The first four weeks of work shall be considered a trial
    period. After the trial period, both parties shall affirm their
    intention for a full year of employment by initialing this
    paragraph: Nanny _____ date _____ .
    Employer _____ date _____ .

2. Nanny Responsibilities

    A. To provide child care up to _____ hours per day,
    _____ days per week. Child care includes: Planning and
    involving the Children in daily activities and routines that
    nurture their physical, emotional, social, and intellectual

development; attending to Children's personal hygiene and dressing; planning and preparing nutritious meals and snacks for Children; observing Children's health and development and keeping Employer informed, and caring for Children when they are ill.

B. To keep daily logs of each child's day and communicate with Employer promptly about any special child- or work-related problem or concern.

C. To comply with employer's discipline and childrearing preferences.

D. To perform light housekeeping duties as follows: Doing the children's laundry and simple repairs/alterations; cleaning and tidying Children's bedrooms/bathrooms/playroom; making Children's beds and care/cleaning/storage of bed and bath linens/spreads/blankets for Children's rooms; maintaining Children's equipment and toys in clean and safe condition; keeping Children's closets/drawers/shelves tidy; cleaning up in kitchen after each use; shopping for Children's food/clothing/sundries as requested by Employer; assisting Employer with reorganization of Children's rooms/clothing/other effects from time to time.

E. To make appointments for Children as requested by Employer (doctor, dentist, hairdresser, etc.).

F. To transport Children when and where needed and run child-related errands.

G. To care for the Children while traveling.

H. To be a good role model for the Children.

I. To contribute to a good working/living relationship with others in the household.

J. To work cooperatively with others concerned with the children's well-being (example: family, teachers, health professionals).

K. To provide reasonable flexibility in the event of an emergency or other unusual circumstance.

3. Work Schedule

Nanny shall be on duty up to _____ hours per week using the following guidelines:

A. Normally, hours of duty will be from _____ to _____ five days per week.

B. Normally, the Nanny's days off will be _____ and _____ .

C. Occasional periods of 24-hour-per-day work may be scheduled as mutually agreed by the parties.

D. Overtime hours can be scheduled as mutually agreed by the parties; however, Nanny burnout is not in anyone's best interests and excessive overtime should be avoided.

E. Reasonable accommodation will be made for the personal needs of both parties.

F. Times and days can be rescheduled and adjusted by mutual agreement and shall be adjusted for emergencies.

G. Times and days for periods of travel with the Children will be handled on an individual basis.

4. Compensation

Employer agrees to pay Nanny a base salary of $_____ per week, payable weekly on _____ . The base salary will be increased to $_____ per week on _____ . The base salary shall cover the normal on duty hours per week provided for in paragraph 3 even if less hours are actually worked due to scheduling, Children spending time with parents or other responsible persons, vacations, holidays, or other approved reasons. Overtime pay shall be $_____ per hour, which is one and one-half times the Nanny's current hourly rate. Nanny shall be entitled to one paid vacation day for each month worked, vacation to be scheduled as mutually agreed. Paid holidays will be as follows: New Year's Day, Memorial Day, Independence Day, Labor Day, Thanksgiving Day, Christmas Day, other _____ . Nanny shall be provided appropriate meals and snacks while on duty. Nanny shall be reimbursed for reasonable personal costs and expenditures on behalf of the children while on duty. When Nanny travels as part of her/his duties, all travel expenses will be paid for by the Employer and salary and overtime, if applicable, paid as usual. Benefits shall include (example: health insurance, continued education): _____

_____.

5. Government Requirements

    Employer shall comply with social security/medicare and tax requirements (federal, state, and local) and shall withhold appropriate amounts from payments to Nanny. Employer will _____/will not _____ pay Nanny's portion of the required social security/medicare tax. Employer will comply with applicable workers' compensation, unemployment compensation and Fair Labor laws.

6. Transportation (check A or B, whichever is applicable)

    _____ A. Employer shall provide a car for Nanny's use when on duty and shall pay for travel expenses, including insurance, maintenance, parking, tolls, and gas. Nanny is responsible for keeping the car interior reasonably neat and clean.

or _____ B. Nanny shall provide transportation for the children as needed when on duty. Employer shall pay for travel expenses including parking and tolls and shall reimburse Nanny for mileage at the rate of _____ cents per mile. Nanny shall obtain insurance coverage for business use of his/her car, and Employer shall reimburse Nanny for the additional cost of this coverage.

7. Living Arrangements (check A or B, whichever is applicable)

    _____ A. Nanny shall live in and be provided room and board as follows:

a. Full board (all meals, snacks, and other foods consumed by Nanny) including specially requested items up to $_____ per week.

b. Employer agrees to provide accommodations up to _____ days per week.

c. Areas considered Nanny's private accommodations are as follows: _____

_____ .

Such areas _____ are/ _____ are not open to any of Nanny's guests without specific permission from Employer. Nanny will keep such areas reasonably neat. Cleaning such areas will be done by _____ Nanny/ _____ household staff. Nanny may personalize such areas as follows: _____

_____ .

d. "Common areas" are as follows: _____

_____

_____ .

These areas may be used by Nanny _____ at any time, _____ whenever not occupied by Employer or Employer's guests, _____ whenever Employer is not at home, _____ only when Nanny is working.

e. Common areas may be used to entertain Nanny's guests _____ at any time, _____ when not occupied by employer, when Employer is not at home, _____ with employer's permission only, _____ not to be used by Nanny to entertain guests, _____ other: _____

_____ .

_____ B. Nanny shall live out. Nanny may be reached by telephone at _____ .

9. Respect of Private Areas and Property

A. Both parties will respect the privacy of the other by knocking and waiting to be asked to enter any private area. This includes the Children with regard to entering Nanny's private areas.

B. Private property of one party may not be used by the other until permission and any necessary instructions have been given.

10. Meetings and Evaluations

A. Nanny and Employer shall meet at least weekly to discuss child- and work-related matters.

B. After the first three and six months of work, Employer shall provide Nanny with written job performance evaluations and salary review. Thereafter, meetings with written evaluation and salary review shall occur at least every six months.

11. Termination of Contract

A. During the first four weeks of employment, a one-week notice of termination is required from either party, or Employer may terminate Nanny with one week of severance pay.

B. After the first four weeks of employment, the Employer must either give four weeks notice of termination, or terminate Nanny with four weeks of severance pay.

C. After the first four weeks of employment, if Nanny decides to leave the position, Nanny will provide at least four weeks notice of termination. No severance pay is required if Employer then wishes to terminate before the end of the four-week period.

D. Notwithstanding the above, if Nanny is terminated for gross negligence or misconduct, no notice is required, but Nanny shall be entitled to one week of severance pay.

E. At the time of Nanny's termination, any outstanding bills incurred by Employer on behalf of Nanny may be deducted from Nanny's pay.

12. Other Terms: (Example: swimming supervision, pet care, use of telephone, use of Employer's car for personal transportation, sick days, supervision of other household staff, additional house rules and policies, etc.)
(Use the reverse side of this page if necessary.)

Date: _____ Sign: _____

NANNY

Sign: _____

EMPLOYERS

Daily Care Records

DAILY CARE RECORD (Infant)			
Child	Date	From A.M./P.M.	To A.M./P.M.
Parent instructions			

Feedings

Time Fluid (type & amt.)   **Solids** (type & amt.)   **Comments**

Diaper changes (note anything unusual in elimination)

Activities (time and type)

Outings

	Time	**Comments**
Bath		
Naps		
Bedtime		

Comments/Observations on development, health, habits, etc.

DAILY CARE RECORD (Toddler/Preschooler)

Child	Date	From	To
		A.M./P.M.	A.M./P.M.

Parent instructions

Meals/Snack (time and food eaten)

Breakfast   Fluids _____ oz.

Lunch   Fluids _____ oz.

Dinner   Fluids _____ oz.

Snacks   Fluids _____ oz.

Comments

Diaper changes/toileting (comment as appropriate)

Activities (time and type)

Outings

	Time	Comments
Bath		
Naps		
Bedtime		

Comments/Observations on development, health, habits, etc.

Appendix C

Nanny Job Performance Evaluation

Nanny: _____ Date: _____

CHILD CARE	Outstanding	Good	Fair	Poor
Maintains an environment that nurtures child's self esteem and sense of security.	—	—	—	—
Communicates effectively with child.	—	—	—	—
Provides appropriate guidance and discipline.	—	—	—	—
Plans and provides developmentally appropriate activities.	—	—	—	—
Maintains a safe, healthy, and comfortable environment for child.	—	—	—	—
Provides physical care safely and skillfully.	—	—	—	—
Interacts with child while providing physical care.	—	—	—	—

CHILD CARE (cont.)	Outstanding	Good	Fair	Poor
Maintains child's clothing appropriately (laundry, repair; keeps closets/drawers tidy).	—	—	—	—
Plans and prepares nutritious meals and snacks for child.	—	—	—	—
Handles emergencies appropriately.	—	—	—	—
Provides appropriate care to sick child.	—	—	—	—

PROFESSIONALISM

	Outstanding	Good	Fair	Poor
Shows interest in work with children.	—	—	—	—
Approaches work in an organized way.	—	—	—	—
Shows ability to work without supervision.	—	—	—	—
Works cooperatively with parents and others concerned with child's well-being.	—	—	—	—
Contributes to a good working/ living relationship with others in the household.	—	—	—	—
Communicates with parents regularly and effectively on matters concerning the child and other job-related matters.	—	—	—	—
Discusses problems constructively.	—	—	—	—
Handles new situations effectively.	—	—	—	—
Displays tact; respects privacy of employer.	—	—	—	—

PROFESSIONALISM   Outstanding   Good   Fair   Poor
   (cont.)

Is dependable in attendance
and punctuality.   —   —   —   —

Provides a positive role model
to children.   —   —   —   —

COMMENTS

Date   Nanny's signature   Employer's signature

Appendix D

Resources for Nannies

Professional Associations

International Nanny Association
    Station House
    900 Haddon Avenue
    Collingswood, NJ 08108
    609-858-0808

National Association for the Education of Young Children
    1509 16th Street NW
    Washington, DC 20036-1426
    1-800-424-2460

National Association of Nannies
    7413 Six Forks Road, Suite 317
    Raleigh, NC 27615
    1-800-344-6266

Periodicals

Child Health Alert, P.O. Box 610228, Newton Highlands, MA 02161. (Easy-to-read and published monthly, this newsletter summarizes and comments on recent health research and issues.)

Nanny News, P.O. Box 2005, Delray Beach, FL 33447-2005. (A bimonthly newsletter for in-home child-care professionals and their employers.)

Parents Pediatric Report, Box 155, 77 Ives Street, Providence, RI 02906. (Practical health information for child-care providers. Eleven issues per year and index).

Note: The professional associations listed above each publish a journal or newsletter for their members.

Legal Information and Advice

Depending on the situation, the agencies listed below may be contacted for help with questions about legal rights or obligations or legal representation. Check the telephone directory or your community resource guide for the local office.

American Civil Liberties Union

County Department of Human Services—child protection services

Equal Employment Opportunity Commission

Legal Aid Society

Prosecutor's Office—county or city

State Civil Rights Commission

State Child Care Licensing Bureau—usually a division of the department of human services or health

Women's Law Fund

Additional Local Resources

American Heart Association, local chapter (CPR courses)

American Red Cross, local chapter (CPR, first aid, and water safety courses)

County Board of Mental Health (mental health services and programs)

Local health department (immunization and screening programs, environmental health, prenatal and infant health)

Local hospitals (may offer fitness, weight-control and other health-promotion programs; newsletters with health updates and tips)

Local police department (child safety, home security)

Poison Control Center (poison prevention and emergencies)

Rape Crisis Center (personal safety)

United Way Information and Referral Service

Note: Additional resources are listed in Appendix F, with emphasis on those serving children and families.

Appendix E

Annotated Book List
for Nannies

The following list provides a sampling of books to consider for your professional library, or for further reading about topics relevant to your particular employment situation. Books to use with children are suggested under some topics.

CHILD CARE

Allen, K.E., and Marotz, L. (1994). *Developmental Profiles: Prebirth to Eight*, second edition. Albany, NY: Delmar Publishers.

Provides the underlying knowledge of development necessary for caring for young children. Concise and easy to follow. Includes typical routines and activities at each stage.

Arena, J.M., and Bacher, M. (1978). *Child Safety Is No Accident*. Durham, NC: Duke University Press.

Uses a developmental approach to accident prevention. Covers many dangers in many situations. A valuable resource for anyone responsible for child safety.

Bassett, M. (1995). *Infant and Child Care Skills*. Albany, NY: Delmar Publishers.

A practical guide to children's health and everyday physical care from birth on, in a clear, step-by-step format. Written for today's caregiver, this hands-on book covers such topics as nursery hygiene; safety and comfort; newborn care; daily care for infants, toddlers, and preschoolers; recognizing illness and care of the mildly ill child at home; and travel with children. Emphasizes the link between skilled physical care and the young child's overall development.

Berman, C., and Fromer, J. (1991). *Meals Without Squeals*. Palo Alto, CA: Bull Publishing Co.

A child-care feeding guide that includes nutrition basics, menus, recipes, and special problems. Practical and readable, this book is intended for caregivers.

Boston Children's Hospital (1987). *The New Child Health Encyclopedia*. New York: Dell Publishing Co.

A parent's guide to keeping children healthy and dealing with injury and illness. Contains useful, easy-to-find information for anyone working with children from birth to adolescence.

Brazelton, T.B. (1992). *Touchpoints*. New York: Addison-Wesley Publishing Co.

A comprehensive, practical reference for understanding and supporting a child's emotional and behavioral development. Includes special topics such as loss and grief, divorce, hospitalization, and television, as well as the typical challenges of childhood.

Bredekamp, S. (Ed.) (1997). *Developmentally Appropriate Practice in Early Childhood Programs Serving Children from Birth through Age 8*, revised edition. Washington, DC: National Association for the Education of Young Children.

Guidelines for quality early education and care that have application wherever young children are cared for.

Faber, A., and Mazlish, E. (1980) *How to Talk So Kids Will Listen and Listen So Kids Will Talk*. New York: Avon.

An enthusiastic action approach to communicating with children and helping them solve their own problems.

Mayesky, M. (1995). *Creative Activities for Young Children*, fifth edition. Albany, NY: Delmar Publishers.

A wealth of ideas and activities for nurturing children's creativity in developmentally appropriate ways. Although this text focuses on group care, material is adaptable for use at home or other settings.

Miller, K. (1985). *Ages and Stages: Developmental Descriptions and Activities Birth Through Eight Years*. West Palm Beach, FL: Telshare Publishing Co.

Short, clear descriptions of young children's abilities and needs combined with a range of activities appropriate to nurturing emerging skills. Samples of simple, homemade materials are suggested.

Miller, K. (1984). *Things to Do with Toddlers and Twos*. West Palm Beach, FL: Telshare Publishing Co.

Based on a respectful understanding of the toddler, this book offers a wide range of activities, designs for toys, and techniques to use in nurturing toddlers at home or in group care. Also available, *More Things to Do With Toddlers and Twos* (1990).

Mitchell, G. (1982). *A Very Practical Guide to Discipline with Young Children*. West Palm Beach, FL: Telshare Publishing Co.

Gentle, positive discipline techniques for a wide range of common situations. Emphasizes the importance of consistency and the development of strong, positive self-image.

Riley, S.S. (1984). *How to Generate Values in Young Children*. Washington, DC: National Association for the Education of Young Children.

For parents and caregivers, examples and guidance about treating children in ways that promote the characteristics we want them to develop.

Sawyers, J.K., and Rogers, C.S. (1988). *Helping Young Children Develop Through Play*. Washington, DC: National Association for the Education of Young Children.

Practical suggestions for caregivers and parents.

Warren, R.M. (1983). *Caring: Supporting Children's Growth*. Washington, DC: National Association for the Education of Young Children.

A concise guide to helping children deal with the challenges of growing up, including divorce, death, and abuse.

DIVERSITY

Dernan-Sparks, L., and the A.B.C. Task Force (1989). *Anti-Bias Curriculum: Tools for Empowering Young Children*. Washington, DC: National Association for the Education of Young Children.

Many suggestions for helping caregivers and children respect each other as individuals and for overcoming barriers based on race, gender, culture, or ability. Includes holiday activities.

Jalango, M.R. (1988). *Young Children and Picture Books: Literature from Infancy to Six*. Washington, DC: National Association for the Education of Young Children.

In addition to providing a useful guide to book selection and reading techniques, this practical resource suggests literature for children that celebrates cultural diversity and the universality of human experience.

Jenkins, J. (1979). *Growing Up Equal: Activities and Resources for Parents and Teachers of Young Children*. Englewood Cliffs, NJ: Prentice Hall.

Practical ideas for teaching the value of diversity.

McWhirter, M.E. (Ed.) (1970). *Games Enjoyed by Children Around the World*. Philadelphia, PA: American Friends Service Committee.

Fun activities for introducing children to other cultures.

Neugebauer, B. (1992). *Alike and Different: Exploring Our Humanity with Young Children* (revised edition). Washington, DC: National Association for the Education of Young Children.

A book for exploring the unique qualities of individuals and helping children to understand and value diversity.

Rappaport, L. (1986). *Recipes for Fun: Play Activities and Games for Young Children with Disabilities and their Families*. Washington, DC: Let's Play to Grow.

A resource for parents and caregivers of children with disabilities.

Schneidewind, N., and Davidson, E. (1983). *Open Minds to Equality: A Source Book of Learning Activities to Promote Race, Class and Age Equity*. Englewood Cliffs, NJ: Prentice-Hall.

Practical suggestions for promoting respect for others as individuals.

Books to Use with Children

Brinn, R.E. (1984). *More Let's Celebrate: Fifty-Seven All-New Jewish Holiday Crafts for Young Children*. Rockville, MD: Kar-Ben Copies, Inc.

A hands-on guide to celebrative crafts and activities.

Charette, B.R. (1981). *The Story for Chanukah for Children*. Milwaukee, WI: Ideals Publishing Corp.

The history and customs of the Jewish December holiday, Chanukah (or Hanukkah).

Chocolate, D.M. (1992). *My First Kwanzaa Book*. New York: Scholastic Books.

An introduction to the African American December holiday of Kwanzaa.

Fisher, A. (1985). *My First Hanukkah Book*. Chicago, IL: Children's Press.

An introduction to the Jewish holiday of Hanukkah.

Françoise (F. Seignobosc) (1953). *Noël for Jeanne-Marie*. New York: Scribner's.

A Christmas celebration.

Galbreath, N. (1984). *The Story of Passover for Children*. Milwaukee, WI: Ideals Publishing Corp.

The history and customs of the Jewish holiday, Passover, celebrated in the spring.

Kindersley, B., and Kindersley, A. (1995). *Children Just Like Me*. Chattanooga, TN: U.S. Committee for UNICEF.

Introduces readers to many aspects of children's daily lives around the world. Full-color photographs and lots of information.

Nathan, J. (1987). *The Children's Jewish Holiday Kitchen*. New York: Schocken Books.

Designed for cooking with children, this book is helpful in understanding Jewish holidays, their meaning, customs, and special foods.

Woods, P., and Liddell, F. (1996). *Merry Christmas, Baby.* New York: Harper-Collins.

A family treasury for Christmas and Kwanzaa.

Yolan, J. (1996). *Milk and Honey.* New York: G.P. Putnam's Sons.

Poems, songs and stories for the Jewish year, with illustrations and explanations.

DUAL-CAREER PARENTING

Brazelton, T.B. (1985). *Working and Caring.* Reading, MA: Addison-Wesley.

Ideas about being a high quality parent as well as a working parent.

A NEW SIBLING

Lansky, V. (1984). *Welcoming Your Second Baby.* New York: Bantam Books.

Practical suggestions for helping a first child adjust to a new sibling. Includes special circumstances such as adoption, half-siblings, twins, and the newborn who is ill or premature.

Books to Use with Children

Cole, J. (1985). *The New Baby at Your House.* New York: William Morrow and Co. (ages 2–6)

Describes activities and changes involved in having a new baby in the house and the feelings experienced by older siblings.

Lansky, V. (1990). *A New Baby at Koko Bear's House.* Deephaven, MN: Book Peddlers. (ages 2–6)

An illustrated story for children with tips for parents to prepare for a new baby's arrival and keep the older child's self-esteem intact.

Rogers, F. (1985). *The New Baby.* New York, NY: G.P. Putnam's Sons. (ages 2–6)

Explains the needs of toddlers faced with a new baby in the family and some of the changes and disruptions the baby can cause in the life of the older sibling.

ADOPTION

Lancaster, K. (1996). *Keys to Parenting an Adopted Child*. Hauppage, NY: Barron's.

A practical, informative guide to raising an adopted child. Includes helpful resources in the appendices.

Melina, L.R. (1986). *Raising Adopted Children*. New York: Solstice Press.

A manual for adoptive parents.

Watkins, M., and Fisher, S. (1993). *Talking with Young Children about Adoption*. New Haven, CT: Yale University Press.

Guidelines for addressing the concerns young children have with being adopted.

Books to Use with Children

Girard, L. (1986). *Adoption Is for Always*. Niles, IL: Albert Whitman and Co. (ages 3–6)

Although Celia reacts to having been adopted with anger and insecurity, her parents help her accept her feelings and celebrate their love for her by making her adoption day a family holiday. Includes factual information about adoption.

Girard, L.W. (1989). *We Adopted You, Benjamin Koo*. Niles, IL: Albert Whitman and Co. (ages 6–11)

Nine-year-old Benjamin Koo Andrews, adopted from Korea as a baby, describes what it is like to grow up adopted in another country.

Keller, H. (1991). *Horace*. New York: Greenwillow Books. (ages 3–6)

Horace, an adopted child, realizes that being part of a family depends on how you feel, not on how you look.

Miller, K.A. (1994). *Did My First Mother Love Me?* Buena Park, CA: Morning Glory Press. (ages 4–8)

Addresses some of the questions children ask about being adopted.

Schnitter, Jane (1991). *William Is My Brother*. Indianapolis, IN: Perspective Press. (ages 3–8)

Two young boys are the same in many ways except that one was born into the family and the other was adopted.

For a free catalog of books about adoption, call Tapestry Books 1-800-765-2367.

DIVORCE, SINGLE PARENTS, STEPFAMILIES

Brazelton, T. Berry (1989). *Families: Crisis and Caring*. Reading, MA: Addison-Wesley Publishing Co.

Practical suggestions for coping effectively with challenges commonly encountered by today's parents and children.

Burt, M.S., and Burt, R.B. (1983). *What's Special About Our Step-family?* Garden City, NY: Dolphin Books.

A participation book for children in stepfamilies.

Grollman, E. (1969). *Explaining Divorce to Children*. Boston: Beacon Press.

A guide for parents.

Lansky, V. (1996). *Divorce Book for Parents* (3rd revised edition). Deephaven, MN: The Book Peddlers.

A comprehensive and practical guide for helping children deal with divorce and its aftermath. Covers a wide range of related topics including legal aspects, information for when one parent is gay, books for children, and other helpful resources.

Maltes, J. (1994). *Single Mothers By Choice*. New York: Times Books.

A guidebook for single women who are considering or have chosen motherhood.

Pickhardt, C. (1996). *Keys to Single Parenting*. Hauppage, NY: Barron's.

Covers a wide range of concerns and challenges for the parent who is divorced, abandoned, or widowed.

Visher, E., and Visher, J. (1982). *How to Win as a Stepfamily*. New York, NY: Dembner Books.

Practical suggestions for becoming a successful stepfamily.

Books to Use with Children

Brown, L., and Brown, M. (1986). *The Dinosaurs Divorce*. Boston, MA: Little, Brown. (ages 3–6)

Simple explanations of various aspects of divorce for young children. Comic-style illustrations.

Christiansen, C.B. (1995). *My Mother's House, My Father's House*. New York: Atheneum Books. (ages 3–6)

Deals with a child's feelings when she lives part of the time with her mother and part with her father.

Girard, L. (1988). *At Daddy's On Saturdays*. Niles, IL: Albert Whitman. (ages 6–10)

Katie's daddy moves away. It seems a long time to Saturday when she sees him, but her mother and her teacher help her until the day arrives.

Goff, B. (1969). *Where is Daddy?* Boston: Beacon Press. (ages 3–6)

A little girl is confused and frightened by her parents' divorce and the changes it brings to her life. By the end of the story, she has begun to adjust.

Mayle, P. (1988). *Why Are We Getting a Divorce?* New York: Crown Publishing. (ages 6–10)

This illustrated book deals with difficult topics and feelings of loss with humor and sensitivity.

DEATH

Fitzgerald, H. (1992). *The Grieving Child*. New York: Simon and Schuster.

A comprehensive, practical resource for helping children with their grief.

Goldman, L. (1994). *Life and Loss: A Guide to Help Grieving Children*. Washington, DC: Taylor and Francis.

Practical information, hands-on activities, and resources, including an annotated bibliography, for adults helping children deal with grief.

Grollman, E. (1976). *Explaining Death to Children*. Boston: Beacon Press.

A difficult topic is addressed in a thoughtful, straightforward way.

Schaefer, D., and Lyons, C. (1986). *How Do We Tell the Children?* New York: Newmarket Press.

Covers many situations when parents and other caring adults need guidance for helping children understand and cope with death. A simple, straightforward resource.

Berg, S., and Lasker, J. (1981). *When Pregnancy Fails: Families Coping with Miscarriage, Still-Birth, and Infant Death*. Boston: Beacon Press.

Two parents who lost babies provide their perspective to a personal loss.

Books to Use With Children

Hammond, J. (1981). *When My Daddy Died* and *When My Mommy Died*. Cincinnati, OH: Cranbrook Press. (age 3 and up)

Simple text and illustrations for the young child who has lost a parent.

Johnson, J., and Johnson, M. (1982). *Where's Jess?* Omaha, NE: Centering Corp. (ages 3–5)

Answers to a young child's questions about her baby sister who has died.

Johnson, J., and Johnson, M. (1990). *Tell Me Papa*. Omaha, NE: Centering Corporation. (ages 8 and up)

Clear, simple answers to children's questions about death, burial, cremation, and saying good-bye.

Rogers, F. (1991). *So Much to Think About*. Pittsburgh, PA: Family Communications, Inc. (ages 3–6)

An activity book that provides hands-on ways for young children to commemorate the death of a person they have loved.

Viorst, J. (1971). *The Tenth Good Thing about Barney*. New York: Athaneum. (ages 6 and up)

A comforting story about loss and remembering when a child's cat dies.

For a free catalogue of books about loss and grief for adults and children, write to: Centering Corporation, 1531 N. Saddle Creek Road, Omaha, NE 68104, or telephone: 402-553-1200.

CHILD ABUSE

Besharov, D. (1990). *Recognizing Child Abuse*. New York: The Free Press/Macmillan.

An informative, practical resource for parents, professionals, and anyone concerned about identifying, reporting, and preventing child abuse and neglect.

Matsakis, A. (1991). *When the Bough Breaks: A helping guide for parents of sexually abused children*. Oakland, CA: New Harbinger Publications.

A resource for parents when sexual abuse has occurred.

Miller, K. (1996). *The Crisis Manual for Early Childhood Teachers*. Beltsville, MD: Gryphon House.

A guide for handling various difficult problems when working with children and families. Includes violence, natural disasters, divorce, and death.

ADULT HEALTH

The American Medical Women's Association (1995). *The Women's Complete Health Book*. New York: Delacorte Press.

A comprehensive guide to women's health.

The Boston Women's Health Book Collective (1992). *The New Our Bodies, Ourselves*. New York: Simon and Schuster.

Informative and comprehensive, this book is designed to help women take charge of their health and be informed consumers of health care.

Reader's Digest (1994). *Great Health Hints and Handy Tips*. Pleasantville, NY: Reader's Digest Association, Inc.

A reference guide covering diet, lifestyle, disease prevention, and family health.

Simon, H. (1992). *Staying Well*. New York: Houghton Mifflin Co.

Comprehensive guide to developing and maintaining a healthy lifestyle.

WARDROBE PLANNING

Coffey, B., and the Editors of *Glamour* (1979). *Glamour's Success Book*. New York: Simon and Schuster.

Wardrobe Planning for the job, at home, in the community, and everywhere.

Dolce, D., with DeVellard, J.P. (1983). *The Consumer's Guide to Menswear*. New York: Dodd, Mead and Co.

Tips for recognizing top quality in everything from shoes to suits and how to get best value for shopping dollars.

Heloise (1985). *Heloise's Beauty Book*. New York: Arbor House.

Practical advice on personal care routines and selection and care of clothes.

Pooser, D. (1985). *Always in Style*. Washington, DC: Acropolis Books Ltd.

A woman's guide to choosing clothes.

ETIQUETTE

Baldridge, L. (1990). *The New Manners for the 90's*. New York: Rawson Associates.

Comprehensive, common-sense guide to contemporary good manners in many situations.

Hoving, W. (1961). *Tiffany's Table Manners for Teenagers*. New York: Ives Washburn, Inc.

This short, illustrated classic takes the mystery out of table etiquette and stresses considerate behavior toward others. Available from Tiffany's.

Post, E.L. (1987). *Emily Post on Etiquette*. New York: Harper and Row Publishers.

A pocketbook guide that provides answers to the most frequently asked questions about manners in everyday life.

DOMESTIC SKILLS

Rhoads, G., and Paradis, E. (1988). *The Woman's Day Help Book.* New York: Viking Penguin, Inc.

A guide to maintaining a clean, healthy, organized home environment. Covers a wide variety of topics arranged in alphabetical order.

Florman, M., and Florman, M. (1993). *How to Clean Practically Everything* (3rd edition). Yonkers, NY: Consumer Reports Books.

A handy reference for easy, inexpensive and safe cleaning methods and products, including a stain-removal chart.

Publications on many topics relevant to in-home child care are also available from:

Consumer Information Center
Pueblo, CO 81002

(Write for a free catalog of government publications on many topics.)

National Association for the Education of Young Children
1509 16th Street NW
Washington, DC 20036-1426
1-800-424-2460

(Write or call for a free catalog of early childhood resources)

Appendix F

Resources for Services to Children and Families

Many organizations have local agencies. Your local United Way information and referral service may be the first place to contact for help with a referral to an agency appropriate to the particular interest or situation.

FAMILY AND PARENTING

Adoptive Families of America
3333 Hwy 100 N
Minneapolis, MN 55422
1-800-372-3300
(support, assistance, and information for adoptive parents)

American Academy of Child and Adolescent Psychiatry
3615 Wisconsin Avenue NW
Washington, DC 20016
1-800-333-7636

American Academy of Pediatrics
P.O. Box 927
Elk Grove Village, IL 60009-0927

Association for the Care of Children's Health
7910 Woodmont Avenue, Suite 300
Bethesda, MD 20814
(books, journals, pamphlets for adults and children)

American Association of Marriage and Family Therapy
1133 15th Street NW, Suite 300
Washington, DC 20005

The Compassionate Friends
P.O. Box 3696
Oak Brook, IL 60522
(self-help organization for parents who have experienced the death of a child)

Gifted Child Society
190 Rock Road
Glen Rock, NJ 07452

National Organization of Mothers of Twins
P.O. Box 23188
Albuquerque, NM 87192-1188

National SAFE KIDS Campaign
111 Michigan Avenue, NW
Washington, DC 20010
(safe environments for children at home and in the community)

Parents Without Partners
401 N. Michigan Avenue
Chicago, IL 60611
1-800-637-7974

Single Mothers by Choice
P.O. Box 1642
Gracie Square Station
New York, NY 10028

Stepfamily Association of America
215 Centennial Mall S., Suite 212
Lincoln, NE 68508

BIRTH DEFECTS

American Cleft Palate Association
1218 Grandview Avenue
Pittsburgh, PA 15211

The ARC (formerly the Association for Retarded Citizens)
500 E. Border Street, Suite 300
Arlington, TX 76010
(advocacy and programs for children and adults with mental
retardation; prenatal health)

Cystic Fibrosis Foundation
6931 Arlington Road, No. 200
Bethesda, MD 20814

Exceptional Parent
1-800-247-8080
(magazine for parents of children with disabilities; publishes an
annual resource guide as well as specialized articles in its regular issues)

March of Dimes Birth Defects Foundation
1275 Mamaroneck Avenue
White Plains, NY 10605
(prenatal health)

Spina Bifida Association of America
4590 MacArthur Boulevard NW, Suite 250
Washington, DC 20007-4226

United Cerebral Palsy Association
1522 K Street, NW
Washington, DC 20005

CONDITIONS AND DISEASES

American Diabetes Association
1660 Duke Street
Alexandria, VA 22314
1-800-232-3472

American Foundation for the Blind
11 Penn Plaza, Suite 30
New York, NY 10001
1-800-AFB-LINE

American Speech-Language-Hearing Association
10801 Rockville Pike
Rockville, MD 20852
(language development, hearing screening/disorders)

American Lung Association
1740 Broadway
New York, NY 10019-4374
(respiratory diseases, tuberculosis)

Asthma & Allergy Foundation of America
1125 15th Street NW, Suite 502
Washington, DC 20005

Epilepsy Foundation of America
4351 Garden City Drive
Landover, MD 20785

Juvenile Diabetes Foundation
120 Wall Street
New York, NY 10005
1-800-JDF-CURE

National Alliance for the Mentally Ill
200 N. Glebe Road, No. 1015
Arlington, VA 22203
1-800-950-NAMI

National Association for Parents of the Visually Impaired
P.O. Box 317
Watertown, MA 02272
1-800-562-6265

Sickle Cell Disease Association of America
200 Corporate Pointe, Suite 495
Culver City, CA 90230
1-800-421-8453

SIDS Alliance
1314 Bedford Avenue, Suite 210
Baltimore, MD 21208
1-800-221-SIDS
(Sudden Infant Death Syndrome information; support for parents bereaved by SIDS)

LEARNING DISORDERS

Learning Disabilities Association of America
4156 Library Road
Pittsburgh, PA 15234

Orton Dyslexia Society
Chester Bldg., Suite 382
8600 LaSalle Road
Baltimore, MD 21286
1-800-ABCD-123

CHILD ABUSE AND DOMESTIC VIOLENCE

Child Abuse Registry
1-800-342-9152
(for parents whose child has been sexually abused; referrals to professional help)

National Center for Assault Prevention
606 Delsea Drive
Sewell, NJ 08080
1-800-258-3189
(training in child abuse prevention through the Child Assault Prevention (CAP) program)

National Center for Missing and Exploited Children
2101 Wilson Boulevard, Suite 550
Arlington, VA 22201
1-800-843-5678

National Coalition Against Domestic Violence
P.O. Box 18749
Denver, CO 80218
(information about state contacts and shelters)

National Committee to Prevent Child Abuse
322 S. Michigan Avenue, Suite 1600
Chicago, IL 60604
1-800-394-3366
(parenting publications; operates Healthy Families America program)

National Council on Child Abuse and Family Violence
115 Connecticut Avenue NW, Suite 400
Washington, DC 20036
1-800-222-2000

Parents Anonymous
675 W. Foothill Boulevard, Suite 220
Claremont, CA 91711
(child abuse prevention through support for overstressed parents; self-help programs, hotlines and information nationwide)

Survivors of Incest Anonymous
P.O. Box 21817
Baltimore, MD 21222
(support and self-help recovery program for adults who were victims as children)

DRUG ABUSE

Al-Anon Family Groups
P.O. Box 862
Midtown Station
New York, NY 10018
1-800-356-9996
(for relatives and friends of individuals with a drinking problem; operates Al-Ateen for those 12–20 years affected by someone else's drinking)

Alcoholics Anonymous (AA)
475 Riverside Drive
New York, NY 10163

American Council for Drug Education
c/o Phoenix House
164 W 74th Street
New York, NY 10023
1-800-488-DRUG (24-hour telephone)

Children of Alcoholics Foundation
P.O. Box 4185
Grand Central Station
New York, NY 10163
1-800-359-COAF

Families Anonymous, Inc.
P.O. Box 3475
Culver City, CA 90231
1-800-736-9805
(support for parents and friends of children with substance abuse or behavior problems)

National Council on Alcoholism and Drug Dependence
12 W. 21st Street
New York, NY 10010
1-800-NCA-CALL

National Parents' Resource Institute for Drug Education
10 Park Place S, Suite 540
Atlanta, GA 30303

ADDITIONAL LOCAL RESOURCES

Board of Education

Child Abuse Hotline

County Board of Mental Health

County Board of Mental Retardation and Developmental Delay

Domestic Violence Hotline

Health Department

Parent-Teacher Association (PTA)

United Way Information and Referral Service

Glossary

Definitions are generally limited to their usage within this text and do not necessarily include all uses of a term.

abrasion: Superficial injury to skin or mucous membrane from scraping or rubbing.

adolescence: Period of human development between onset of puberty (sexual maturity) and the beginning of adulthood.

advocate: One who speaks or acts in support of another's cause.

anorexia nervosa: Eating disorder characterized by self-imposed starvation and persistent denial of any appetite for food.

attachment: An affectionate bond that develops between a child and another person and that joins them emotionally.

au pair: Person who lives as part of a host family in a foreign country to experience the culture and improve skills in the country's language in return for helping with child care and housework. French term literally meaning "as an equal."

authoritarian: Parenting style characterized by the use of control and the expectation of unquestioning obedience.

authoritative: Parenting style characterized by firm but reasonable limits, prudent guidance, and respect for the child's individuality.

autonomy: Sense of independence and the ability to make one's own decisions.

baby blues: Colloquial term used to describe the temporary letdown, miserable feeling commonly experienced by mothers about four days after childbirth.

behavior: Anything that a person does or says that can be observed.

belief: Acceptance that certain things are true.

bias: Prejudice or inclination toward a particular point of view.

body language: Nonverbal communication unconsciously expressed in body movements, gestures, and facial expression.

body mechanics: The various systems of the body working together to maintain balance and posture.

bonus: Payment or other reward given an employee over and above regular compensation.

bulimia: Eating disorder characterized by secretive bingeing (rapid overeating) and purging (such as self-induced vomiting or use of laxatives or enemas).

burnout: Exhaustion resulting from overwork and related **stress**.

calorie: Unit used to measure the energy value of food.

cardiovascular: Pertaining to the heart and blood vessels.

child abuse: Physical, emotional, or sexual mistreatment or assault of a child.

child neglect: Failure of parent or guardian to meet a child's basic needs.

cohabitation: Living together as though married when not legally married.

colleague: Person of the same **profession**.

communication: Giving or exchanging information in any way, such as speech, gestures, writing.

competency: Demonstrable skill and knowledge.

contract: A formal, written agreement between two or more people to do certain things.

courtesy: Polite, gracious, and considerate behavior toward others.

culture: A way of life of a particular group of people encompassing all aspects of life and passed on from one generation to another.

curriculum: A plan for learning.

custody: Legal responsibility for the care, protection, and nurture of a child.

custom: A social practice passed on by tradition.

demeanor: Way of conducting oneself.

development: Series of changes that occur with passing time in an orderly sequence and with the integration of biological and environmental factors.

dignity: Sense of proper pride in who one is and what one does.

discipline: Guidance that leads a child toward socially acceptable behavior and self-control.

egalitarian: Pertaining to the belief in equal access to political, economic, and social rights for all.

employment agreement: An arrangement between an employer and employee with respect to the terms of employment.

environment: Physical, cultural, and behavioral conditions that surround and influence an individual.

ethics: Code of conduct of a particular person, profession, religion, or other group.

etiquette: Rules of acceptable social behavior.

ethnic: Pertaining to a group of people distinguished by a common history, customs, language and other shared characteristics.

extended family: Family unit consisting of parents, children, grandparents and other relatives such as aunts and uncles.

facial tic: Minor involuntary muscular movement or twitching of face which may be associated with a psychological factor.

failure to thrive: Malnourished, underweight condition of infancy; many causes, but often associated with inadequate feeding and stimulation.

fetal alcohol syndrome: Birth defects resulting from excessive maternal alcohol consumption during pregnancy. Defects may include small head, small eyes, delayed development, and abnormalities of joints, limbs or organs such as the heart. Also referred to as FAS.

governess: A woman employed by a family as a teacher to educate school-age children at home. Male equivalent: **tutor.**

grief: Intense emotional pain and sadness resulting from a significant loss or other extremely distressing event.

gross salary: Total salary before deductions.

health: State of physical, mental, and social well-being.

hives: Eruption of itchy welts on the skin caused by reaction to an allergic substance in food, medication, or by direct skin contact.

humanities: Fields of learning concerned with human thought and relationships, such as literature, philosophy, history, and languages.

hygiene: The study of health and the practice of measures to promote and maintain health.

Industrial Revolution: Profound changes in social and economic organization, beginning in England around 1760, as machines replaced hand tools and large-scale industrial production developed.

industrialization: Process of organizing a society and economy based on large industries and machine production.

infant: Imprecise term, but usually refers to a child during the first year of life, after which the toddler emerges.

integrity: Quality of uncompromising honesty and moral principle.

kindergarten: Educational program to prepare young children, usually about age five, for school; term is German for "children's garden."

laceration: A wound or irregular tear of the skin or other tissue.

lifestyle: A person's way of life, exemplified by his or her possessions, activities, attitudes, and manner.

mandated: Required, ordered.

manners: Polite behavior in accordance with social conventions and consideration for others.

Middle Ages: The period of European history between ancient and modern times, from about the fifth to the fifteenth century A.D.

middle childhood: Stage of development between preschool and **adolescence**, from about six to twelve years of age.

multicultural: Culturally diverse; coming from various different cultures.

nanny: In-home caregiver employed by a family, either on a live-in or live-out basis, to perform all tasks related to the care of young children. Implies a caregiver with special training or considerable experience. Sometimes referred to as a child's nurse.

newborn: The infant during the first four weeks after birth. Also called a neonate.

nursery nurse: Title given in Great Britain to a person who has received special training and is qualified to care for young children in group settings as well as private homes.

nutrient: Substance or component of food; has specific uses in the body.

nutrition: The study of food and how it is used by the body. Also, the sum total of all the processes by which food is taken in and used by the body for survival, growth, and repair.

objectively: Describes unprejudiced, detached perception that is independent of one's own subjective thoughts and feelings.

paraphernalia: Drug supplies and equipment such as: pipes, cigarette papers, roach clips, aerosol cans, pills, powder, crushed brown leaves, capsules, glue tubes, beer or liquor containers.

permissive: Parenting style characterized by little parental guidance or direction.

perquisite: An extra benefit or privilege accompanying a job. Sometimes referred to colloquially as a perk.

personal hygiene: Personal habits contributing to health, such as handwashing, bathing/showering, care of teeth, nails and hair, and wearing clean clothes.

philosophy: A particular set of principles for guiding conduct.

postpartum: Occurring after childbirth.

posture: Position of the body.

practicum: A course in which a student gains practical experience in a field of study.

prenatal care: Medical supervision of a pregnant woman and the fetus.

principle: A rule of right conduct.

probation: A trial period.

profession: An occupation requiring special preparation and **competencies**.

professional: One who engages in an occupation requiring special preparation and **competencies**; pertaining to a **profession**.

professional detachment: A state of being impartial and impersonal in professional situations.

professionalism: A quality of conduct and skills that is worthy of a **profession**.

regression: A return to an earlier stage of development in response to a stressful situation.

regressive behavior: Renewal of behavior from which a child had developmentally advanced, such as toileting accidents, thumb sucking, or wanting a bottle.

ritual: A traditional procedure or ceremony.

rocker: Servant hired to rock the baby's cradle.

role model: A person whose behavior serves as an example to others and inspires them to copy the behavior.

self-esteem: How a person feels and thinks about himself or herself.

self-respect: Proper respect for one's worth as a person.

self-worth: How a person values himself or herself.

sex role: Societal or cultural characteristics (masculine or feminine) of one's gender.

Shaken Baby Syndrome: Head injury in an infant resulting from forceful shaking.

skeletal: Pertaining to the body's bony framework, the skeleton.

social class: Group of people ranked together in society according to economic, educational, and occupational criteria.

socialization: The process of learning to become an acceptable member of the society in which one lives.

social sciences: The study of people and society in such fields as sociology, psychology, political science, and economics.

socioeconomic: Involving both social and economic factors.

status: Position or rank, as in society.

stress: Tension in response to a physical, mental or emotional demand on the body.

suffrage: The right to vote in political elections.

tutor: A man employed by a family as a teacher to educate school-age children at home. Female equivalent: **governess**.

unethical: Not conforming to an expected code of conduct or moral standards.

value: A social **principle** or standard held or accepted by an individual, class, or society.

Victorian: Characteristic of the period when Victoria was queen of England, 1837–1901.

visa: An endorsement on a passport authorizing entry into a particular country.

wet nurse: A woman employed to breastfeed another woman's baby.

Index

273